Design and Development of Efficient Multipath Routing Protocol in Mobile Ad-hoc and Sensor Networks

Dr.J . Viji Gripsy

Dr. Anna Saro Vijendran

Published by

Design and Development of Efficient Multipath Routing Protocol in Mobile Ad-hoc and Sensor Networks

ISBN 978-93-86176-02-8

Authors

Dr.J . Viji Gripsy

Dr. Anna Saro Vijendran

Bonfring

309, 2nd Floor, 5th Street Extension, Gandhipuram,

Coimbatore-641 012.

Tamilnadu, India.

E-mail: info@bonfring.org

Website: www.bonfring.org

Phone: 0422-3928700

Acknowledgement

First and foremost I thank **GOD** almighty for guiding me to complete my work successfully.

I am highly indebted to express my heartfelt, sincere and eternal gratitude to my Ph.D Supervisor, **Dr. Anna Saro Vijendran**, Director, Department of Computer Application, SNR Sons College, Coimbatore for her constant support, inspiration and valuable guidance during the course of my research work. It has been an honor for me to be her first Ph.D. student. The joy and enthusiasm she had for research was contagious and motivational for me, even during tough times in the Ph.D. pursuit. I appreciate all her contributions of time, ideas that made my Ph.D. experience productive and stimulating. Her affection for me is fondly remembered. I am really blessed to have her guidance for my future research and academic career.

I express my deep sense of gratitude to the Managing Trustee **Mr.R. Vijayakumhar**, S.N.R Sons College for given me an opportunity to pursue my research in their esteemed institution.

I extend my sincere thank to the former Principal and Secretary **Dr.V. Sengodan**, S.N.R Sons College for permitting me to do this research.I record my gratitude to the Principal and Secretary **Dr.H. Balakrishnan**, S.N.R Sons College who gave me the opportunity and support to carry out this fruitful research.

I wish to express my gratitude to the management of **Smt. Nandini Rangaswamy**, PSGR Krishnammal College for Women, Coimbatore who allow me to do my research work.

I am very thankful to **Dr.(Mrs.)N. Yesodha Devi,** Secretary, PSGR Krishnammal College for Women, Coimbatore for her valuable suggestions for my research.

I am grateful and indebted to **Dr.(Mrs.) S. Nirmala**, Principal, PSGR Krishnammal College for Women, Coimbatore for her valuable guidance and support. And also I thank my colleagues and friends who have willingly helped me to do the best.

I owe and respectfully offer my thanks to my beloved husband **D.Jebaseelan Selvakumar**, my children **Jerson** and **Jersha** for their constant moral support and mellifluous affection which helped me to achieve success in every sphere of life and without their kind devotion this research work would have been a sheer dream. Finally, I render my sincere thanks to my Mother, Father, Brother and Teachers for their prayers and never ending support.

Dr.J . Viji Gripsy

Author's Profile

Dr.J. Viji Gripsy

Assistant Professor

Department of Computer Science

PSGR Krishnammal College for Women

Coimbatore

Dr.J. Viji Gripsy, M.Sc., M.Phil., Ph.D., She is an Assistant Professor in the Department of Computer Science in PSGR Krishnammal College for Women, Coimbatore, India. She is having teaching experience of 10 years in the field of Computer science. Her area of Specialization is Security in Mobile Adhoc and Wireless Sensor Networks. She has presented more than ten papers in various National and International Conferences in India and Malaysia. Also she has published several papers in International journals. She has received her Ph.D Degree from Bharathiar University under the guidance of Dr. Anna Saro Vijendran in SNR Sons College, Coimbatore, India. She is currently member in Universal Association of Computer and Electronics Engineers (UACEE) and International Association of Engineers (IAENG).

Dr. Anna Saro Vijendran

Director

Department of Computer Applications

SNR Sons College

Coimbatore

Dr. Anna Saro Vijendran, M.C.A., M.Phil., Ph.D., She is the Director in Department of Computer Applications, SNR Sons College, Coimbatore, India. She has rich teaching experience of 23 years in the field of Computer science. Her areas of specialization are Digital Image Processing and Artificial Neural Networks .She has presented more than 30 Papers in National and International Conferences held in various places like Cairo, Singapore, Malaysia. She has published more than sixty eight papers in International Journals. She is presently guiding research scholars leading to Ph.D degree in Anna University, Bharathiar University, Manonmaniam Sundaranar University and Karunya University. She holds various positions such as Reviewer for reputed Journals, Session Chair in International conferences.

<table>
<tr><td>**Chapter**</td><td>**Contents**</td><td>**Page No**</td></tr>
</table>

CHAPTER 1

INTRODUCTION

1.1. Introduction to the Study

Mobile Ad hoc Networks (MANETs) is a self-configuring decentralized network that utilizes self organization of communication between potentially moving nodes and thus the network topology changes constantly. In the past three decades great amount of research has been carried out in the MANET field. Due to extent knowledge gained from MANETs, Researchers are now trying to apply this expertise to the field of Wireless Sensor Networks (WSN). The main reason is that both MANETs and WSNs are self-configurable networks of nodes connected by wireless links. Compared to MANETs, the WSNs technology resources are inadequate and hence more research work is required to develop the WSN to overcome the demerits in the traditional protocols and networking algorithms. Great care should be taken before applying MANET algorithms, protocols and techniques in WSNs that were originally developed for MANETs. Although both types of networks have many similarities, while designing for WSN the differences also to be taken into account for better adaptability and suitability. The subsequent section describes about the common similarities and differences among MANETs and WSNs.

1.1.1. Similarities between MANETs and WSNs

The wireless ad hoc networks were initially developed and used by the US defense. WSNs resemble ad hoc network in the sense that both are having distributed wireless networks and routing between two nodes involves intermediate relay nodes known as multi hop routing. Besides both ad- hoc and sensor nodes are usually battery powered and therefore there is a big concern on minimizing power consumption. In addition, both networks use a wireless channel placed in an unlicensed spectrum that is prone to interference by other radio equipments operating in the same frequency. Also self-management is required because both networks are distributed in nature. Recently there is a re-emergence of advanced ad hoc networks resulting in smaller more powerful mobile devices and emergence of new types of ad hoc applications. Higher chip configuration and hardware architectures optimized for low power operation equipped with new ultra wideband (UWB) and multiple input multiple output (MIMO) radios take advantage of wider unlicensed spectrum creating new type of mobile devices with remarkable capabilities.

New applications are changing the face of traditional ad hoc networks (i.e., pure routing) to advanced networks where networking, processing, and storage could be done everywhere in the network.

1.1.2. *Differences between MANETs and WSNs*

Even though the WSNs and MANETs have significant similarities there are also fundamental differences. The key differences arise from the nature of its network types. Generally, MANETs are used in devices such as laptops, personal digital assistant (PDA) and mobile radio terminals. Conversely, the sensor networks that are handled by human focus on interacting with the environment. As a consequence, the number of nodes as well as the density of deployment in sensor networks is of higher magnitude than in ad hoc networks. The vision of seminal projects such as SmartDust (Kahn et al. 1999) contemplates networks with thousands or millions of nodes, though the largest deployment till date has about 800 nodes.

If a network is going to be deployed in outdoors, in the middle of the forest or in the middle of the ocean, or in the hills, some nodes will eventually get damaged and fail. This means that the topology of the network will change dynamically, not due to node mobility as in ad hoc networks but due to failure of some nodes. In this case reconfiguration mechanisms will have to be used such that the network design should consider those nodes which are prone to failure. There are some applications where nodes are related to animals, cars or moving objects. But in the majority of applications, nodes remain static. The issues that are important in mobile networks may not be of great importance in wireless sensor networks. Besides failure, topology may also change due to the sleep-awake cycle observed in some protocols designed with sensor networks. These protocols go through these cycles in order to achieve energy savings, which is one of the biggest concerns and design requirements in resource-scarce sensor networks.

This scarcity of resources constitutes a differentiating feature in sensor networks. Nodes are typically left unattended for long periods of time (i.e., months, years) in sensor networks which operate on batteries. The range of communications is typically within a few meters and at low rates (some kilobits per second). Also memory is of few kilobytes and the operating speed of the processor is a few megahertz.

It should also be pointed out that the service offered by wireless sensor networks is not simply to move bits from one place to another, but to provide answers instead. These answers should respond to questions such as: what are the regions of the network whether the temperature is above the specified threshold? What is the path followed by the herd? Thus, responding to these types of questions implies taking into account geographic scopes, which is a requirement that is not needed in most other networks. Indeed, in some applications the ID (e.g., the address) of individual nodes is irrelevant and location becomes a more important attribute. In general, communication paradigms are affected by the application-specific nature of sensor networks.

1.2.   Research Background

A design suitable for both MANETs and WSNs is known as Mobile Ad-hoc and Sensor Networks (MASNETs).In this research, routing protocol is considered for evaluation in MASNET. Besides, common design principle is regarded for better adaptability and suitability. In the following sections terminologies related to this research are briefly described.

Infrastructure Less: Central servers, specialized hardware and fixed routers are necessarily absent. The lack of such infrastructure precludes the deployment of centralized host relationships. Instead, nodes uphold egalitarian relationships. This means that any security solution has to rely on a distributed cooperative scheme instead of a centralized scheme.

Wireless Link Use: Wireless link usage renders ad hoc networks susceptible to attacks. In wired networks, an adversary gain physical access to the network wires or pass through several lines of defense at firewalls and gateways whereas attacks on a wireless ad hoc network can come from all directions and target any node. Hence ad hoc network does not have a clear line of defense and every node have to be prepared to defend against threats. Moreover, the MAC protocols used in ad hoc networks, such as IEEE 802.11 rely on trusted cooperation in a neighborhood to ensure channel access, which leads to high vulnerability.

Multi-hop: Because of the lack of central routers and gateways, hosts are themselves routers. Thus packets follow multi-hop routes and pass through different mobile nodes before arriving at their final destination. Due to the possible untrustworthiness of such nodes, this feature presents a serious vulnerability.

Node Movement Autonomy: Mobile nodes are generally autonomous units that are capable of roaming independently. This means that tracking down a particular mobile node in a large scale ad hoc network is not simple.

Amorphous: Node mobility and wireless connectivity allow nodes to enter and leave the network spontaneously to form and break links unintentionally. Therefore, the network topology has no fixed form regarding both its size and shape. Any security solution has to take this feature into account.

Power Limitation: Ad hoc enabled mobile hosts are small and lightweight and they are often supplied with limited power resources, such as small batteries. This limitation causes vulnerability, in the sense that attackers may target some nodes batteries to disconnect them which may lead to network partition. This is called an energy starvation attack or sleep deprivation torture attack. This feature also represents a challenging constraint while designing security solutions.

Memory and Computation Power Limitation: Ad hoc enabled mobile nodes have limited storage devices and weak computational capabilities. Consequently, high complexity security solutions, such as symmetric or asymmetric data encryption are difficult to implement. Mobile devices used in ad-hoc networks are lightweight and portable. Hence the devices and the information stored in the devices can be easily stolen. Mechanisms for protecting both devices and information have to be employed.

1.2.1. *Threats*

The threats that can affect the security of ad hoc networks are classified into two classes, attacks and misbehaviour (Djenouri et al 2005; Yau and Mitchell 2003).

Attacks

Attacks include any action that intentionally aims to cause any damage to the network. They can be divided according to their origin or their nature. An origin-based classification splits attacks into two categories, external and internal, whereas a nature based classification splits them into passive and active attacks (Yau and Mitchell 2003).

External Attacks: Includes attack launched by a node that does not belong to the logical network or the node which is not allowed to access the network.

Internal Attacks: Includes attacks launched by an internal compromised or malicious node. This is a severe type of threat since the defense mechanisms proposed for an external attack is ineffective against the internal compromised or malicious nodes.

Passive Attacks: A passive attack is a continuous collection of information that might be used later when launching an active attack. The attacker eavesdrop packets and analyzes them to pick up required information. Due to the nature of the wireless communication medium which is widely shared, it is easier for an attacker to launch such an attack in wireless environment than in traditional wired environments. The security attribute that have to be provided here is information confidentiality.

Active Attacks: An active attack is a network exploit in which a hacker attempts to make changes to data on the target or data en route to the target. Includes almost all other attacks such as sleep deprivation torture, which targets the batteries hijacking in which the attacker takes control of a communication between two entities and masquerades as one of them jamming which causes channel unavailability by overusing it, attacks against routing protocols etc. Most of these attacks result in a denial of service (DoS), which degrades or halts the communication between nodes completely.

Misbehavior

Misbehavior is defined as an unauthorized behavior of an internal node that results unintentional damage to other nodes. The aim of the node is not to launch an attack but it may have other aims such as obtaining an unfair advantage compared with the other nodes. For instance, one may not correctly execute the MAC protocol with the intent of getting higher bandwidth or it may refuse to forward packets for others to save its resources, while using their resources and asking them to forward its own packets (Hu and Perrig 2004). This is not an intentional attack but a selfish behavior. However it represents a potential danger that threatens the quality of service in the network as well as one of the most important network security requirements (Yokoyama et al 2006).

1.2.2. Security Requirements

The security services of mobile ad hoc networks have to ensure that the network is protected as equivalent to wired network. The main objective of these services is to protect information and resources from attacks and misbehavior. In dealing with network security, the following requirements are to be ensured by using well designed security architecture (Djenouri et al 2005; Yau and Mitchell 2003).

Availability: Ensures that the desired network services are available whenever they are expected in spite of the presence of attacks. Systems that ensure availability in MANET have to overcome denial of service and energy starvation attacks, as well as node misbehavior such as node selfishness in packet forwarding.

Authentication: Ensures that the communication from one node to another is genuine. In other words, it ensures that a malicious node does not masquerade as a trusted network node.

Data Confidentiality: Ensures that a given message is not understood by anyone other than its intended recipient. Data confidentiality is typically enabled by applying symmetric or asymmetric data encryption.

Integrity: The authenticity of data sent from one node to another. It ensures that a message sent from node A to node B is not modified by any malicious node C during its transit.

Non-repudiation: In computer networks, non-repudiation is the ability to ensure that nodes do not deny the sending of a message that it originated.

1.2.3.   Multipath Routing

Standard routing protocols in ad hoc wireless networks, such as AODV (Bogdanoski, M., Suminoski, T., & Risteski, A., 2013) and DSR (Maquelin, O., Gao, G. R., Hum, H. H., Theobald, K. B., & Tian, X. M. 1996) develop a single route between source and destination node. When the developed route fails, the source needs to discover a new route to the destination. This new route discovery will result in additional packet delay and network overhead. Multipath routing attempts to find and simultaneously maintain multiple routes between a source and destination node. When the first active path (possibly representing the shortest delay path) fails, a new alternative path to the destination can be immediately used. The benefits of multipath routing include

Optimal Paths Utilization: By ranking paths by some (possibly time-varying) metrics, optimal paths for packet transmission can be selected at any given time.

Load Balancing: By distributing traffic over multiple routes, congestion and bottlenecks between nodes due to limited bandwidth can be mitigated.

Fault-tolerance: By sending the same packet along all discovered routes, higher degree of fault-tolerance can be achieved. The destination node can successfully receive the packet as long as at least one of the routes does not fail. Obviously, this broadcasting approach is not bandwidth efficient.

Higher Aggregate Bandwidth: By utilizing all discovered routes simultaneously to route split packets, higher aggregate bandwidth can be achieved. In this research work, optimal paths utilization and load balancing have been considered. A novel traffic allocation strategy based on pheromone concept and its applications is presented.

1.3. Research Motivation

The wireless network is given more importance for more than a decade which ensures growth and development in the network. Wireless network offers a greater comfort for people, the government and social organisation and has an immense future in the real world. Since this network is closely associated with real world, security consideration finds a major role. Many researchers have already confirmed the chances of misbehaving nodes in the ad hoc and wireless networks. The misbehaving nodes in an ad hoc and wireless network results in degradation of the overall network throughput and creates difficulty in finding routes between nodes. Thus the collaborative nature of ad hoc network seems to be endangered due to the presence of misbehaving nodes and even get worse when the nodes collude to misbehave. So, it creates a need for designing a new mechanism to minimize such false detections and avoid nodes misbehaviour.

Since the beginning of computer network history, routing mechanism has relied on the knowledge of nodes address in order to establish path between them. MANETs follow a traditional node-centric behaviour for routing and its routing mechanism is primarily classified into three types known as proactive, reactive and hybrid. WSNs generally behave on data-centric and application-centric nature. Thus pure node-centric feature may fail to give better performance on sensor networks. Main objective of MASNET is to capitalize the optimum efficiency from both MANETs and WSNs.

Multipath routing attempts to find and simultaneously maintain multiple routes between a source and destination node. Several multipath routing algorithms have been found in the literature and the authors address the problems in the existing algorithms or methods. A recent proposal by Bayrem Triki et al., 2012 has exhibited a secure multipath routing algorithm, which allows nodes in mobile ad-hoc and sensor networks to perform an on-demand discovery and generation of a set of paths. The authors have proposed an algorithm known as Secure Multipath Routing Algorithm for Mobile and Sensor Networks (SeMuRAMAS) which is adaptive, secure and uses labels to carry the disjointness threshold between nodes during the route discovery. But the proposal lacks efficiency on broadcasting scheme, which has motivated to investigate and implement broadcasting scheme in MASNETs.

1.4. Research Objectives

SeMuRAMAS proposal mainly relies on k-x connectivity for disjointness threshold. It broadcasts the Route Request (RREQ) to overall nodes in the network and makes all nodes to save all information regarding possible routes from the source node to itself and thus routing overhead is unavoidable. This research is mainly intended to design and develop a broadcasting scheme and evaluate its impact on the quality of service.

The following objectives are drafted to achieve betterment.

- To enhance the broadcasting scheme with respect to multipath routing
- To ascertain the adaptability of Location Aided Routing (LAR) protocol in Quadrant Based Routing (QRS) Scheme.
- To examine the rectangular zone approach in association with LAR.
- To consolidate the best possible combination of broadcasting scheme to enhance the efficiency with respect to energy efficiency, routing overhead and packet delivery ratio.

1.5. Research Contribution

In this research work, the following four multipath routing protocols in MASNET have been developed.

- Dynamic Multipath Routing Protocol (DMPR) which is an extension of Multipoint Relay (MPR) and is primarily concerned about the security and selective broadcasting mechanism.
- Quadrant Based Routing (QRS) Scheme is a quadrature form of broadcasting scheme which incorporates the capability of Location Aided Routing (LAR) along with security enhancement on node misbehaviours.
- Rectangular Zone based Location Specific Routing (RZLSR), an extension of LAR which broadcast the route discovery in tilted rectangular zone.
- Adaptive Secure Multipath Routing (ASMR) a new broadcasting proposal which combines the power of DMPR and RZLSR for route discovery and route maintenance phase along with security mechanism.

1.6.   Evaluation Setup

NS-2 is a discrete event simulator developed by the University of California at Berkeley and the VINT project. It has established itself as a prominent environment for studying TCP and other protocols over networks like the conventional wired Internet. Simulator is used for simulation of routing protocols, among others, and is heavily used in ad-hoc networking research, and supports popular network protocols, offering simulation results for wired and wireless networks.

1.7.   Organization of the Research Work

Chapter 1   Describes the MANET & WSN, research motivation, research objectives, security, multipath routing and thesis overview.

Chapter 2   Exhibits various reviews related to ad hoc & wireless networks, routing scheme, secure multipath routing and attacks.

Chapter 3   It describes the theoretical overview of secured multipath routing in mobile ad-hoc and wireless sensor networks.

Chapter 4   Deals with collective issues of SeMuRAMAS, Multipoint Relay based broadcasting scheme DMPR and its performance evaluation.

Chapter 5   Portrays the new broadcasting scheme based on Location Aided Routing (LAR) and its exclusive performance evaluation with SeMuRAMAS.

Chapter 6   Introduces the Rectangular based routing scheme (RZLSR) for secure multipath routing in MASNET. Extensive simulation is carried out and the results are presented.

Chapter 7   Explores the collaborative approach of our preceding proposals and its best part known as Adaptive Secure Multipath Routing (ASMR). The performance evaluation is shown.

Chapter 8   Explains the common findings extracted from this thesis and consolidate it as conclusion. Further, scope for future direction is also discussed.

Chapter 9   Pictures the performance evaluation of the proposed secure multipath routing scheme with the other routing scheme for MASNET.

CHAPTER 2

REVIEW OF LITERATURE

2.1. Introduction

The node misbehaviour problem in wireless network has been studied by many researchers **(Haas 1997; Lin et al 1997; Rodoplu 1999; Zhang et al 2003)**and various techniques have been proposed to prevent node misbehaviour on data forwarding. These schemes are broadly classified into two categories Mobile Ad Hoc Network and Wireless Sensor Network.

Royeret al (1999) has proposed an ad hoc mobile network which is a collection of mobile nodes that are dynamically and arbitrarily located in such a manner that the interconnections between nodes are capable of changing on a continual basis. This article examines routing protocols for ad hoc networks and evaluates these protocols based on a given set of parameters. The author provides an overview of eight different protocols by presenting their characteristics and functionality and compares and discusses their respective merits and drawbacks.

Lada Jr, H.F. (2000) examines an audio power management system for a computer to eliminate noise signals associated with the power-down and power up operations of the computer. The audio power management system asserts a speaker mute signal before power is removed from the amplifier to reduce transient conditions.

Conti, M., Maselli, G., Turi, G., & Giordano, S. (2004) have proposed a strict layered design which is not flexible enough to cope with the dynamics of MANET environment and prevents performance optimizations. The Mobile Man cross-layer architecture offers an alternative to the pure layered approach that promotes stricter local interaction among protocols in a MANET node.

Ferri, R., Kim, M., & Yee, E. (2004) have proposed a system which comprises a plurality of motes, each mote having a sensor and a wireless communication system for communicating with neighbouring motes, a distributed routing table distributed amongst each of the plurality of motes and an update system for periodically updating the distributed routing table.

Yick et al (2008) explore the design of a WSN which depends significantly on the application and it considers factors such as the environment, the application's design objectives, cost, hardware and system constraints. The authors give an overview of several new applications and then review the literature on various aspects of WSNs. They classify the problems into three different categories: internal platform and underlying operating system, communication protocol stack, and network services, provisioning, and deployment. They review the major development in these three categories and outline new challenges.

Tanejaa, S., Kushb, A., Makkarc, A., & Bhushand, B. (2011) have proposed a scheme that takes into consideration the power awareness during route selection. This scheme observes power status of each and every node in the topology and further ensures the fast selection of routes with minimal efforts and faster recovery.

Chen et al (2011) has proposed a traditional mobile wireless network whose design focuses on ubiquitous access and large capacity. In this article, the author has developed a framework for green radio research and integrates the fundamental issues that are currently scattered. The skeleton of the framework consists of four fundamental tradeoffs: deployment efficiency-energy efficiency, spectrum efficiency-energy efficiency, bandwidth-power, and delay-power.

Biswal et al (2011) has studied Dynamic Source Routing (DSR) its characteristics and performances. The study improves DSR that is applied to many other new routing protocols. The improvement is done in route reply (RREP) method. During route reply when more than one route replies are about to reach the source there are high chances that they create congestion at the last point. This congestion is a cause for possible collisions.

2.2. MANET and WSN

Millberg, M., Nilsson, E., Thid, R., Kumar, S., & Jantsch, A. (2004) review the communication protocol stack to be used in Nostrum, Network on Chip (NoC) architecture. In order to aid the designer in the selection of protocols and their respective facilities, a layered approach to communication is taken. A nomenclature for describing the individual layers' interfaces and service definitions of the layers in the protocol stack is suggested and used. The concept includes support for best effort traffic packet delivery as well as support for guaranteed bandwidth traffic using virtual circuits. Further an application to NoC adapter is defined as part of the Resource to Network Interface and is used to communicate between the Nostrum protocol stack and the application. An industrial example has been implemented, simulated and the results justify the suggested layered approach.

Kong, J., Cui, J. H., Wu, D., & Gerla, M. (2005) explains Large-scale underwater ad-hoc networks (UANET) and underwater sensor networks (UWSN) which are novel networking paradigms to explore the uninhabited oceans. In this paper the authors adopt a top-down approach.. At each layer a set of new design challenges is explored. They conclude that UANET and UWSN are challenges that must be answered by inter-disciplinary efforts of acoustic communication, signal processing and mobile acoustic network protocol design

Murphy, A. L., & Picco, G. P. (2006) shows that the notion of transiently shared tale space, originally introduced by the Lime model and middleware to support application development in mobile ad hoc networks, can be successfully applied also to wireless sensor networks (WSNs). While the two scenarios are similar, the peculiar constraints posed by the WSNs (e.g., in terms of resources and energy) require non-trivial adaptations. They describe two models and systems, Tiny Lime and Teeny Lime, providing transiently shared paces in two different WSN operational scenarios and elaborate on alternate designs and opportunities.

Gomez, J., & Garcia-Macias, J. A. (2006) concludes that great care should be taken before applying algorithms, protocols and techniques to WSNs, if they were originally developed for MANETs. They explain the fact that although both types of networks have many similarities, the differences are also such that WSN can arguably be considered as an entirely different research field.

Wu, F. J., Kao, Y. F., & Tseng, Y. C. (2011) reviews the research activities in WSN including networking issues and coverage and deployment issues. Cloud platform and systems (CPS) that have been developed recently, including health care, navigation, rescue, intelligent transportation, social networking, and gaming applications have been received. Through these reviews, it is demonstrated how CPS applications exploit the physical information collected by WSNs to bridge real and cyber space's. They also identified important research challenges related to designs.

Gadallah, Y., & Serhani, M. A. (2011) have proposed service providers that are equipped with lightweight communication devices. In this study, the authors have devised a protocol for the entire operation. They have also experimented with the proposed technique and presented results that show the performance of the service providers under different operating conditions.

Krishna, A. V. (2011) has studied a Mathematical model being used in encryption process, which consumes less power when compared to standard algorithms like Data Encryption Standard (DES) &Rivest-Shamir-Adleman (RSA). The author has studied its strength against noise which is an unavoidable phenomenon within the considered model. The model generates a distributed sequence which is used as sub key. The encrypted form of data during the transmission process will be subjected to errors due to some noise sources

Sigiuk, H. I., & Ihbeel, A. A. (2012) has concluded thatWireless Sensor Network (WSN) is a distinguished Ad Hoc Network that can be used for a specific application. Since a WSN consists of potentially hundreds of low cost, small size and battery powered sensor nodes, it has more potentials than others.

Kumar,P. S., Raghavaiah, B., & Babu, N. S.(2012)have designed and implemented a ZigBee IEEE 802.15.4 platform. Based on an IEEE 802.15.4 radio and ZigBee protocol stack, the developed ITRI ZBnode is an autonomous wireless communication and computing platform aimed at fast prototyping and research in WSNs. The platform attempts to provide a low data rate, low power and low cost wireless networking on the device-level communication. Examples of tree and mesh network formation are provided to demonstrate the developed ZB node platform.

Shirkande, S. D., & Vatti, R. A. (2013) have proposed a colony algorithm inspired from self-organizing behaviour of ants which fall under Swarm Intelligence. In this paper, a survey is done on various ant colony based routing algorithms for Wireless Sensor network (WSN) and Mobile Ad-Hoc Network (MANETs). A comparison of various algorithms is made based on performance metrics, pheromone function to select next node, simulator used, energy awareness, etc.

Hussain, K., Abdullah, A. H., Awan, K. M., Ahsan, F., & Hussain, A. (2013) explains that Wireless Sensor Network (WSN) is an arrangement of sensor nodes to collect environmental data and send it to Base Station (BS). Mobile Ad hoc Networks (MANET) is a network composed of it inerrant nodes via wireless links in deficiency of any infrastructure or topology. Nodes of WSN and MANET are divided into clusters to create a temporary infrastructure for the nodes. A cluster is supervised by a leader node called Cluster Head (CH).The authors present in this paper a wide taxonomy about Cluster Head Selection method in Wireless Sensor Networks.

2.3. Routing Scheme

Schurgers, C., & Srivastava, M. B. (2001) review the optimal routing and tries to maximize the duration over which the sensing task can be performed. They derive a practical guideline based on the energy histogram and develop a spectrum of new techniques to enhance the routing in sensor networks. Their approach aggregates packet streams in a robust way, resulting in energy reduction. They argue that more uniform resource utilization can be obtained by shaping the traffic flow.

Stojmenovic, I. (2002) examines schemes that are loop-free, localized, and which follow a single-path strategy, which are the desirable characteristics for scalable routing protocols. The author explains that routing protocols have two modes: greedy mode (when the forwarding node is able to advance the message toward the destination) and recovery mode (applied until return to greedy mode is possible). Also the methods differ by the metrics used (hop count, power, cost, congestion, etc.) and by past traffic memorization at nodes (memory less or memorizing past traffic).

Carzaniga, A., Rutherford, M. J., & Wolf, A. L. (2004) propose a routing scheme for content-based networking. A content-based network is a communication network that features new advanced communication model where messages are not given explicit destination addresses and where the destinations of a message are determined by matching the content of the message with selection predicates declared by nodes. Routing in a content-based network amounts to propagating predicates and the necessary topological information in order to maintain loop-free and possibly minimal forwarding paths for messages. The routing scheme uses a combination of a traditional broadcast protocol and a content-based routing protocol.

Zhu, J., Qiao, C., & Wang, X. (2004, March) investigates the comprehensive energy consumption models that consider energy consumption for data packets as well as control packets. Based on these models, they propose a minimum energy routing scheme. The simulation results indicate that the scheme performs better than the existing minimum energy routing schemes in terms of energy consumption as well as throughput.

2.3.1. Single Path Routing

Han, H., Shakkottai, S., Hollot, C. V., Srikant, R., & Towsley, D. (2006) describe a scenario where multi-path routing is enabled in the Internet to take advantage of path diversity. Using minimal congestion feedback signals from the routers, they present a class of algorithms that can be implemented at the sources to stably and optimally split the flow between each source-destination pair. They also show that the connection-level throughput region of such multi-path routing congestion control algorithms can be larger than that of a single-path congestion control scheme.

2.3.2. *Multipath Routing*

Nelakuditi, S., & Zhang, Z. L. (2001) have proposed a hybrid approach that uses both globally exchanged link state metrics to identify a set of good paths, and locally collected paths state metrics for proportioning traffic among the selected paths. They compare the performance of their approach with that of global optimal proportions and show that the proposed approach yields near optimal performance using only a few paths. They also demonstrate that the proposed scheme yields much higher throughput with much smaller overhead compared to other schemes based on link state updates.

De, S., Qiao, C., & Wu, H. (2003) describes a meshed multipath routing (M-MPR) protocol with selective forwarding (SF) of packets and end-to-end forward error correction (FEC) coding. They also describe a meshed multipath searching scheme suitable for sensor networks, which has a reduced signalling overhead and nodal database. The performance evaluations show that M-MPR achieves a much improved throughput over conventional disjoint multipath routing with comparable power consumption and receiver complexity and also successfully route a message using FEC coding. Selective forwarding (SF) consumes much less network resources such as channel bandwidth and battery power than packet replication (or limited flooding).

Zafar, H., Harle, D., Andonovic, I., & Khawaja, Y. (2009) proposed a multipath routing scheme, referred to as shortest multipath source (SMS) routing based on dynamic source routing (DSR). The mechanism has two novel aspects compared with other on-demand multipath routing schemes. It achieves shorter multiple partial-dips joint paths and allows more rapid recovery from route breaks. The performance differentials are investigated using NS-2 under conditions of varying mobility, offered load and network size. Experimental results reveal that SMS provides a better solution than the existing source-based approaches in a truly mobile *ad-hoc* environment.

Tarique, M., Tepe, K. E., Adibi, S., & Erfani, S. (2009) investigate the multipath routing protocols for mobile ad hoc networks (MANETs). According to them, the multipath protocols are broadly classified into five categories based on their major goals.

The goals are to improve delay, provide reliability, reduce overhead, maximize network life and support hybrid routing. Issues, objectives, performances, advantages and disadvantages of the protocols are investigated and summarized.

Jaisankar, N., & Saravanan, R. (2010) have proposed a multipath routing scheme which provides better performance and scalability by computing multiple routes in a single route discovery. Also, it reduces the routing overhead by using secondary paths. This scheme computes combination of the node-disjoint path and fail-safe paths for multiple routes and provides all the intermediate nodes of the primary path with multiple routes to destination.

2.4. Secure Multipath Routing

Karlof, C., & Wagner, D. (2003) propose security goals for routing in sensor networks and show how attacks against ad-hoc and peer-to-peer networks can be adapted into powerful attacks against sensor networks, They introduce two classes of novel attacks against sensor networks sinkholes, and HELLO floods and analyze the security of the entire major sensor network routing protocols.They describe crippling attacks them and suggest counter measures and design considerations. This is the first analysis of secure routing in sensor networks.

Bouam, S., & Ben-Othman, J. (2003) explain securing data in ad hoc networks. They exploit the existence of multiple paths between nodes in an ad hoc network to increase the robustness of transmitted data confidentiality. In ad hoc networks, security depends on several parameters and reaching a good security degree is a hard task. An overview of some current solutions, implementation details and experimental results are discussed in this paper.

Kotzanikolaou, P., Mavropodi, R.,& Douligeris, C. (2005)explore several attacks that render multipath routing protocols more vulnerable than it is expected, to collaborating malicious nodes. They propose a novel on-demand multipath routing protocol, the Secure Multipath routing protocol (SecMR) and analyze its security properties. The SecMR protocol can be easily integrated in a wide range of on-demand routing protocols, such as DSR and AODV.

Berton, S., Yin, H., Lin, C., & Min, G. (2006) have studied the problem of secure routing in fully distributed MANETs using multipath routing. After studying the effect of multipath in terms of security, they propose an efficient multipath heuristic and a new approach to protect the route discovery called SDMSR to secure the routing protocol while mitigating security overhead

Mavropodi, R., Kotzanikolaou, P., & Douligeris, C. (2007) identify several attacks that render multipath routing protocols vulnerable to collaborating malicious nodes. They propose an on-demand multipath routing protocol, the secure multipath routing protocol (SecMR), and analyze its security properties. Through simulations, the performance of the SecMR protocol is evaluated in comparison with existing secure multipath routing protocols.

Abduvaliyev, A., Pathan, A. S. K., Zhou, J., Roman, R., & Wong, W. C. (2013) have proposed works on Intrusion Detection Systems (IDS) in WSNs and present comprehensive classification of various IDS approaches according to their employed detection techniques. The three main categories explored in this paper are anomaly detection, misuse detection, and specification-based detection protocols. They give a description of the existing security attacks in WSNs and the corresponding IDS protocols to tackle those attacks. They analyse the works with respect to the network structure of WSNs.

Das, T. (2010) has introduced routing protocols for static networks which are to be redesigned once. This project work addresses the issue of mobility management in wireless ad-hoc network, particularly in mobile ad-hoc network and wireless sensor network. He proposes a routing protocol for wireless ad-hoc networks which handles mobility issue successfully.

Sen, J. (2013) describes that the Wireless sensor networks (WSNs) have attracted a lot of interest in the research community due to their potential applicability in a wide range of real-world practical applications. Various types of attacks on cognitive wireless sensor networks (CWSN) are categorized under different classes based on their natures and targets and corresponding to each attack class, appropriate security mechanisms are also discussed. Some critical research issues on security and privacy in CWSNs have also been identified.

Pushpa Lakshmi, R., & Vincent Antony Kumar (2014) analyze the fuzzy logic method of ant colony optimization (ACO) to establish a secure routing path with minimum delay for mobile ad hoc network. The ACO algorithm is used to establish a virtual backbone connecting cluster heads (CHs). The general ACO algorithm is modified to allow selection of routing path, based on trust value of the nodes lying in the routing path and delaying experienced in the path. The procedure uses a fuzzy logic controller to evaluate the trust value of the nodes based on node's QoS parameters viz. energy drain rate, lifetime of the node, packet drop rate and packet forwarding status of the node. The behavior of the protocol under various attacks is analyzed.

Chandrakant, N. (2014, January) has explained that MANETs are having very limited resources like memory, CPU speed, Bandwidth, battery life etc. In spite of having higher secured nodes and security algorithms sometimes the genuine nodes can be attacked or accessed by fraud malicious nodes. Also he explains that a node itself can turn into malicious behaviour. In such scenarios, it may not be able to trace them to avoid adversary affect or misuse of node's data for other purposes which are dangerous in some cases like Border

Monitoring. As a different approach to avoid such adverse circumstances, this paper is proposes a novel approach to exhaust the valuable resources of MANETs called retiring or invalidating a node.

2.5.   Watchdog Mechanism

Maquelin, O., Gao, G. R., Hum, H. H., Theobald, K. B., & Tian, X. M. (1996) investigate a combined approach Polling Watchdog, where both are used depending on the circumstances. The Polling Watch dog is a simple hardware extension that limits the generation of interrupts to the cases where explicit polling fails to handle the message quickly. As an added benefit, this mechanism also has the potential to simplify the interaction between interrupts and the network accesses performed by the program. They present the performance for the EARTH-MANNA-S system, an implementation of the EARTH (Efficient Architecture for Running TH reads) execution model on the MANNA multiprocessor. In contrast to the original EARTH-MANNA system, this system does not use a dedicated communication processor. Rather, synchronization and communication tasks are performed on the same processor as the regular computations. Therefore, an efficient message-handling mechanism is essential to good performance.

Lee, J. W., Lee, Y. H., & Syrotiuk, V. R. (2007) have proposed two protocols to address the ambiguous collision limitation of watchdogs. The Watchdog Alert (WA) and Watchdog Confirmation (WC) protocols are variants of the Carrier Sense Multiple Access with Collision Avoidance Protocol (CSMA/CA). They analyse the trade-offs between throughput and watchdog success probability of each protocol, comparing it to CSMA/CA.

Sun, B., Osborne, L., Xiao, Y., & Guizani, S. (2007) have described that the intrusion detection systems provide a necessary layer of in-depth protection for wired networks. However, relatively little research has been performed about intrusion detection in the areas of mobile ad hoc networks and wireless sensor networks. In this article, they briefly introduce mobile ad hoc networks and wireless sensor networks and their security concerns and then focus on their intrusion detection capabilities. Specifically, they present the challenge of constructing intrusion detection systems for mobile ad hoc networks and wireless sensor networks, survey the existing intrusion detection techniques and indicate important future research directions.

Chen, H., Wu, H., Cao, X., & Gao, C. (2007, November) explains trust management for WSNs. The main contribution of this work is that they define two kinds of operators, propagation and aggregation which can combine and diffuse trust rating of nodes in WSNs.

Chen, H., Wu, H., Hu, J., & Gao, C. (2008, April) proposes a distributed agent-based trust management scheme. The agent node use watchdog mechanism to observe the behaviour of the sensor nodes and computes the trust rating for them. They consider packet-dropping and hello flood attack in their simulation. The simulation results and analysis show that their scheme can fastly detect the malicious nodes and scale well for wireless sensor networks.

Huang, L., & Liu, L. (2008) explain that watchdog is a kind of behaviour monitoring mechanism which is the base of many trust systems in ad hoc and wireless sensor networks. It is different from the current watchdog mechanisms which only evaluates its next-hop's behaviour and propagates the evaluation result to other nodes by broadcasting, which is neither energy efficient nor attack resilient. An extended watchdog mechanism is proposed in this work. Besides the next-hop, node with extended watchdog will monitor all its neighbours' behaviour on the base of information collected from medium access control (MAC) layer. By overhearing the Clear To Send (CTS) packets, subsequent Request To Send (RTS) or data packets and intervals between them, a node can judge whether its neighbour forwards the packet or not despite the location of the neighbour. The misbehaved node is punished by restricting its injected packets. Analysis and simulations on NS2 prove the effectiveness of extended watchdog mechanism. Its low communication overhead (about 1.76%) and attack resilience resulted from its fully distributed nature makes it a competent solution in constructing a secure wireless sensor network.

Liang, G., Agarwal, R., & Vaidya, N. (2010, March) have proposed a lightweight misbehaviour detection scheme which integrates the idea of watchdogs and error detection coding. They show that even if the watchdog can only observe a fraction of packets by choosing the error detection code properly, an attacker can be detected with high probability while achieving throughput arbitrarily close to optimal. Such properties reduce the incentive for the attacker to attack. He then considers the problem of locating the misbehaving node and proposes a simple protocol, which locates the misbehaving node with high probability. The protocol requires exactly two watchdogs per unreliable relay node.

Sharma, R., Athavale, V. A., & Sharma (2013) explain that an intrusion detection system offers a necessary layer of in-depth protection for wired networks. However, comparatively very little analysis has been performed regarding intrusion detection within the areas of mobile ad-hoc networks and wireless sensor networks. During this article, first the authors tend to introduce mobile ad-hoc networks and wireless sensor networks and their security issues. Then, they tend to concentrate on their intrusion detection capabilities. Specifically, they tends to gift the challenge of constructing intrusion detection systems for mobile ad-hoc networks and wireless sensor networks, survey the prevailing intrusion detection techniques, and indicate vital future analysis directions.

Vidhyapathi, C. M., Sundar, S., Pal, H., & Punia, K. (2013) have explained that AODV (Ad hoc On-demand Distance Vector Routing Protocol). Black hole and Wormhole nodes are malicious nodes which degrade the performance of the network. It actively participates in the network and confirms the forward packets to the destination. The Watchdog Mechanism is used to correct the network from both black hole and wormhole attacks. The networks originally, with the attacks and after being prevented from attacks are compared with the basis of packets received, throughput, end-to-end delay and packet delivery ratio.

Han, G., Jiang, J., Shu, L., Niu, J., & Chao, H. C. (2014) have explored a detailed survey on various trust models that are geared towards WSNs. Then, they analyze various applications of trust models which are malicious attack detection, secure routing, secure data aggregation, secure localization and secure node selection. In addition, they categorize various types of malicious attacks against trust models and analyze whether the existing trust models can resist these attacks or not. Finally, based on all the analysis and comparisons, they list several trust best practices that are essential for developing a robust trust model for WSNs.

2.6. Threshold Signature

Wu, T. S., & Hsu, C. L. (2003) have developed a scheme authentication of the self-certified individual group public keys can be confirmed simultaneously in the procedure of verifying the individual group signatures. As compared with threshold signature schemes which is designed based on the certificate-based public key systems, the developed scheme is more efficient for generating and verifying group signatures in terms of computational efforts and communication costs.

Chang, T. Y., Yang, C. C., & Hwang, M. S. (2004) introduced a(t,n) threshold signature with (k,l) threshold-shared verification to be used in a group-oriented cryptosystem without a shared distribution center (SDC). In this scheme, any participants can represent a group (signing group) to sign a message, and any participant can represent another group (verifying group) to verify the signature. There is no SDC to distribute the public and private keys to all the participants in the two groups. Hence, the scheme is more practical in real-world applications and more efficient than its predecessors in terms of communication and computational complexity and storage.

Glynos, D., Kotzanikolaou, P., & Douligeris, C. (2005, April) have proposed a multifactor authentication framework that extends the cryptographic link, binding an entity to a physical node device. This is achieved using two distinct authentication factors: certified keys and certified node characteristics. Although the proposed framework requires additional sensing capabilities from the MANET nodes, it also provides the additional confidence level required for node authentication in critical applications.

Chai, Z., Cao, Z., & Lu, R. (2007) analyze the threshold password authentication scheme, which meets both availability and strong security requirements in the mobile Ad hoc network, in this scheme. t out of n server nodes can jointly achieve mutual authentication with a registered user within only two rounds of message exchanges scheme allows users to choose and change their memorable password without subjecting to guessing attacks. Moreover, there is no password table in the server nodes end, which is preferable since mobile nodes are usually memory-restricted devices.

Mishra, A. K., & Sahoo, B. (2009) have proposed an extension to Adaptive-SAODV of the secure AODV protocol extension, which includes further filtering strategies aimed at improving its performance. It optimized the routing performance of secured protocols with help of a threshold mechanism.

WANG, P. D., & CHEN, C. Y. (2009) analyze the security framework for mobile agent-ECC (Elliptic Curves Cryptography) model which is selected and constructed. Experiment indicates that this model could effectively reduce network communication time and improve the efficiency and security. And the mobile agent-based WSN communication has ultimately become more secure and effective.

Jhaveri, R. H., Patel, S. J., & Jinwala, D. C. (2012, January) put forward a scheme called Ad-hoc On-demand Distance Vector (AODV) protocol, in which an intermediate node detects the malicious node which sends false routing information. Routing packets are used not only to pass routing information, but also to pass information about malicious nodes. The intended scheme not only detects but also removes malicious node by isolating it, to make safe and secure communication.

D'Souza, R. J., & Varaprasad, G. (2012) have introduced a secure node disjoint multipath routing protocol for wireless sensor networks. Here, the data packets are transmitted in a secure manner by using the digital signature crypto system. It is compared with an ad hoc on-demand multipath distance vector routing protocol. It shows better results in terms of packet delivery fraction, energy consumption, and end-to-end delay compared to the ad hoc on-demand multipath distance vector routing.

Sharma, P. (2012) analyzes the design trusted routing protocols using trusted frame works and intrusion detection system (secure protocol) for MANET. Trust combination algorithms and trust mapping functions are provided in this model, where the former can aggregate different opinions together to get a new recommendation opinion. Based on this trust model, trusted routing protocols for MANET called TAODV on top of Ad Hoc On-demand Distance Vector (AODV) routing protocol is designed.

Singh, M., Babbar, K., & Jain, K. L. (2014) explain that intrusion detection is one of the methods of defending against these attacks. They have presented a survey on various issues and security threats on Wireless Sensor Networks (WSN). They have also discussed the recent trends in Intrusion Detection Systems along with implementation of IDS in WSN and comparative analysis of these schemes.

2.7.   Attacks

Geng, X., & Whinston, A. B. (2000) describes that the active network scan a sign of attackers looking for network weaknesses all over the Internet are harbingers of future Distributed Denial of Service (DDoS) attacks. It signifies the continued dissemination of the evil daemon programs that are likely to lead to repeated DDoS attacks. It gives information about network weaknesses that DDoS attacks exploit the technological futility of addressing the problem solely at the local level, potential global solutions.

Lazos, L., & Poovendran, R. (2004) survey a problem of enabling sensors of WSN to determine their location in an un-trusted environment. Since localization schemes based on distance estimation are expensive for the resource constrained sensors and then proposed a range-independent localization algorithm called SeRLoc. SeRLoc is a distributed algorithm and does not require any communication among sensors. It shows that SeRLoc is a robust against severe WSN attacks like the wormhole attack, the Sybil attack and compromised sensors. It provides a security-aware range-independent localization scheme for WSN.

Mirkovic, J., & Reiher, P. (2004) have conducted two taxonomies for classifying attacks and defences, and thus provide researchers with a better understanding of the problem and the current solution space. The attack classification criteria have been selected to highlight commonalities and important features of attack strategies that define challenges and dictate the design of countermeasures. The defence taxonomy classifies the body of existing DDoS defences based on their design decisions. It then shows how these decisions dictate the advantages and deficiencies of proposed solutions.

Lazos, L., Poovendran, R., & Čapkun, S. (2005) explains about a robust positioning system called ROPE that allows sensors to determine their location without any centralized computation. In addition, ROPE provides a location verification mechanism that verifies the location claims of the sensors before data collection. They proved that ROPE bounds the ability of an attacker to spoof sensors' locations, with relatively low density deployment of reference points. They confirm the robustness of ROPE against attacks analytically and via simulations.

Da Silva, A. P. R., Martins, M. H., Rocha, B. P., Loureiro, A. A., Ruiz, L. B., & Wong, H. C. (2005) describe that the intrusion detection system (IDS) can acquire information related to the attack techniques, helping in the development of prevention systems. They propose an IDS that fits the demands and restrictions of WSNs. Simulation results reveal that the proposed IDS is efficient and accurate in detecting different kinds of simulated attacks.

Tariq, U., Hong, M., & Lhee, K. S. (2006) have analyzed the DDoS problem and simplified taxonomy to categorize the attack scope and available defence solutions. This taxonomy can help the software developers and security practioners to understand the common vulnerabilities which encourages the attackers to launch DDoS attack.

Bing, H. L. H. F. P., & Jing, C. H. E. N. (2006)finds out that the routing protocol will not work for warm hole attacks in MANET. To provide a solution introduced Marsh model. When finding the route, the node will choose the higher trust value neighbour to relay the packet. The model is applied in the Optimized Link State Routing Protocol (OLSR).

Sarma, H. K. D., & Kar, A. (2006) describe about the information in the network which must be protected from the attackers. Attackers may device different types of security threats to make the WSN system unstable. They have identified different types of security threats possible for a sensor net setting. Effort has been made to model the threats mathematically.

Xu, Y., Chen, G., Ford, J., & Makedon, F. (2007) have described about a distributed warm hole detection algorithm for wireless sensor networks, which detects warm hole based on the distortions they create in a network. Wormhole attacks are passive in nature; the algorithm uses a hop counting technique as a probe procedure, reconstructs local maps for each node, and then uses a "diameter" feature to detect abnormalities caused by wormhole.

Znaidi, W., Minier, M., & Babau, J. P. (2008)have reviewed the IDS (Intrusion Detection Mechanism) systems which presents a new WSN attacks ontology that enable to identify the intention of the attacker, its capabilities to achieve the attacks, the target and the end result. This ontology is a high level abstraction that does not depend on the IDS system used. The authors have also surveyed known vulnerabilities and attacks in WSNs and presented some defences.

Nazario, J. (2008)has described that the denial of service (DDoS) attack is designed to overwhelm victims with traffic and to prevent their network resources from working correctly for their legitimate clients. DDoS attacks require a significant amount of bandwidth to successfully attack a big adversary, such as a Web-based media company, so that they often command thousands of hosts in a botnet to simultaneously send traffic to a victim.

Lee, B., Bae, S., & Han, D. (2008) have introduced management platform and security framework for wireless sensor networks. The proposed framework has advantages as regarding secure association and intrusion detection. Further, the proposed mechanism can be applied to ubiquitous application such as u-city, u-healthcare, u-defense as a secure wireless sensor network management platform.

Rehana, J. (2009) has studied the security problems of WSN based on its resource restricted design and deployment characteristics and the security requirements for designing a secure WSN. Also, this study documents the well known attacks at the different layers of WSN and some counter measures against those attacks. The author has discussed some defensive measures of WSN giving focus on the key management, link layer and routing security.

Wu, J., Chen, H., Lou, W., Wang, Z., & Wang, Z. (2010) have analyzed the impacts of wormhole attack on DV-Hop localization scheme. Based on the basic DV-Hop localization process, they have proposed a label-based secure localization scheme to defend against the wormhole attack. The proposed secure localization scheme is capable of detecting the wormhole attack and resisting its adverse impacts with a high probability.

Jaisankar, N., Saravanan, R., & Swamy, K. D. (2010) have proposed that a black hole attack can be working in opposition to routing in mobile ad hoc networks. A black hole node is a malicious node which sends the fake reply route requests and drops the packets. A novel approach is proposed to detect black hole nodes in the MANET .The solution find out the safe route between sending node and receiving node.

Sharif, L., & Ahmed, M. (2010) have examined some of the most common routing attacks in WSNs. They have focused on the warm hole routing attack. A variety of counter measures have been proposed in the literature for such attacks. However, most of these counter measures suffer from flaws that essentially render them ineffective for use in large scale WSN deployments. Due to the inherent constraints found in WSNs, there is a need for lightweight and robust security mechanisms. The examination of the warm hole routing attack and some of the proposed counter measures makes it evident that it is extremely difficult to retrofit existing protocols with defences against routing attacks. It is suggested that one of the ways to approach this rich field of research problems in WSNs could be to carefully design new routing protocols in which attacks such as warmholes can be rendered meaningless.

Modirkhazeni, A., Aghamahmoodi, S., & Niknejad, N. (2011) explains that conventional security mechanisms are not suitable for WSNs as they are usually heavy and nodes are limited. One of the most severe attacks to detect and defend in wireless sensor network is wormhole attack where data will be forwarded from one part of the network to the other part through the wormhole tunnel. They have focused on wormhole attack and proposed distributed network discovery approach to mitigate its effect. This approach can mitigated almost 100% of wormhole attack overload in the environment where 54% of nodes are affected with the wormhole.

Singh, S. K., Singh, M. P., & Singh, D. K. (2011) have investigated the security related issues and challenges in wireless sensor networks. They identified the security threats and reviewed the proposed security mechanisms for wireless sensor networks.

Raote, N. S. (2011) describes that the wormhole attack is possible even if the attacker has not comprised any hosts, and all communication provides authenticity and confidentiality. Using the various approaches for finding the solution over wormhole attack, the dynamic information of the packets could still be modified. In order to give more robust protection in some special scenario like battlefields, which requires highly secured information, there is need of developing some secured mechanism for wormhole detection and prevention. Taking into consideration this problem the proposed scheme is developed. It treats Wormhole attack problem using cryptographic approach i.e. RSA and Multipath routing concept. It improved data security robustly.This approach in wireless Ad-hoc Networks, increasing the transmission speed in security environment. Because, dividing the initial message and exploiting the characteristic of existence of multiple paths between nodes in an Ad hoc network and also increase the robustness of confidentiality

Timcenko, V., & Stojanovic, M. (2012) review in the first part of their work about the comprehensive overview of recent advances in network forensics in MANET environment. In the second part, they have proposed a model of IDS that uses network forensics to detect DDoS attacks in MANET. The forensic analysis relies on inspecting simultaneous malicious activities of a group of attackers(zombies). Since DDoS attack traffic can appear rather alike to legitimate traffic in the sense of bit rate and packet size, the applied method should minimize the risk of misinterpreting legitimate traffic as attack traffic (false positives). The authors propose a flexible IDS model and the associated forensic analysis algorithm based on log file inspection.

Sabahi, F. (2012) explains that thevehicular ad-hoc network (VANET) is a new type of ad hoc network which is becoming even more popular than the original ad hoc concept. The structure of a VANET is built on mobile connectivity between car drivers and automobile equipment that informs the drivers about road status or other necessary travel information. The VANET is capable of improving the safety of the roads and reducing traffic congestion. However, VANETs face security issues are typical of all networks.

Kozlov, D., Veijalainen, J., & Ali, Y. (2012) describe about the development towards the Internet of Things (IoT) and discusses architecture visions for the IoT. The emphasis is to analyze the known and new threats for the security, privacy and trust (SPT) at different levels of architecture. The strong view is that the IoT will be an important part of the global huge ICT infrastructure and humanity will be strongly relying on in the future with relatively few data centers connected to trillions of sensors and other "things" over gateways, various access networks and a global network connecting them.

Dubey, R., Jain, V., Thakur, R., & Choubey, S. (2012) investigates the monitoring of sensitive information such as enemy movement on the battlefield or the location of personnel in a building. They investigate how wireless sensor networks can be attacked in practice.

Bogdanoski, M., Suminoski, T., & Risteski, A. (2013) have analyzed systems vulnerability targeted by TCP (Transmission Control Protocol) segments when SYN flag is ON, which gives space for a DoS (Denial of Service) attack called SYN flooding attack or more often referred as a SYN flood attack. The effects of this type of attack are analyzed and presented in OPNET simulation environment. Further, the authors have proposed two anomaly detection algorithms as an effective mechanism against this type of attack.

Aydip Sen, J. (2013) has conducted a detailed survey on various aspects on security and privacy issues in wireless mesh networks. Future research issue and open problems are also mentioned so that the researchers could find appropriate directions to go ahead with their research works.

Kaur, G., & Dhanda, E. S. K. (2013) has concluded that wormhole attack is one of the severe attacks on wireless sensor network. It tunnels the packets from one end to another end by corrupting it. Routing protocols plays a major role of forwarding the data packets by identifying and maintaining the routes in the network. Competence of sensor networks relay on the strong and effective routing protocol used. The affect of wormhole attack on routing protocols like AODV, DSR, ZRP and ANODR has been analysed with reference to parameters like throughput, delay and energy consumption.

Poddar, G. M., & Rastogi, N. (2014) described about the quantity of this spoofed packet which has been lost in normal traffic and the detection methodology needs to make a clear separation between normal and spoofed traffic. The above functionality is achieved by some traditional methods which work on the concept of Hop Count Filter (HCF) mechanism. But the traditional HCF method only measures the TTL maximum up to 30 hops limit and the packet coming from larger hops will be taken to be spoofed but it was not the case all the time. Sometimes actual packet might come from more hops. Its solution is been drafted as UHCF (Updated Hop Count Filtering) mechanism was suggested.

Chandrakant, N. (2014) explains two scenarios to be considered, scenario-1 is key based communication and scenario-2 is priority based outing and communication. InScenario-1, proposed a novel approach where generated keys are used to authenticate each other by exchanging the keys via unusual paths.Scenario-2 tries to propose a robust algorithm which protects nodes communication in a MANET. For communication with/via a neighbour is based on the neighbors node's priority, here, priority-1 being the highest hence it is highly recommended for communication and priority three is being the lowest and it is rarely recommended for communication. Thisstrategy helps to choose a highly secured route which will help network to have a better communication among its nodes.

Sudha, .C., Rajkumar, D.V.(2014) proposed a wormhole attack resistant secure neighbour discovery (SND) scheme for directional wireless network. The proposed SND scheme consists of three phases: the network controller (NC) broadcasting phase, the network nodes response/ authentication phase and the NC time analysis phase. In the broadcasting phase and the response/authentication phase, local time information and antenna direction information are elegantly exchanged with signature-based authentication techniques between the NC and the legislate network nodes, which can prevent most of the wormhole attacks.

Sandhiya, D., Sangeetha, K., & Latha, R. S. (2014) have explained that routing protocol in MANET operates on the basic assumption that nodes are fully cooperative. Because of open infrastructure and limited battery power some nodes may not cooperate correctly. These nodes start refusing to forward data packets or drop them thereby degrading the performance of network. So it is very essential to develop an Intrusion Detection System (IDS) to prevent MANET from attacks. The IDS Watchdog fails to detect node misbehaviour in the presence of ambiguous collisions, receiver collisions, limited transmission power, false misbehaviour, collusion and partial dropping. An intrusion detection system named Enhanced Adaptive acknowledgment (EAACK) has been developed which consists of three parts, namely, ACK, Secure ACK (S-ACK) and misbehaviour Report Authentication (MRA).

2.8.   Summary

This chapter contains variety of literatures which are reviewed for an enhancement of secured multipath routing in mobile ad-hoc and sensor network environment. The main objective of this research work is to assess the impact of routing scheme on existing secure multipath routing algorithms. Further, mobile ad-hoc attacks, watchdog mechanism and threshold signature are reviewed for its adaptability with new routing scheme. Subsequent chapter explore the significance of secure multipath routing for MASNET

CHAPTER 3

SECURE MULTIPATH ROUTING FOR MASNET

3.1. Introduction

Recently Multipath routing has drawn widespread deliberation in MANETs and WSNs. Due to the cram deployment of nodes in MANETs/WSNs, multipath routing becomes a promising and nature technique to manage the topological changes that occurs frequently and therefore it results in unreliable communication service. Many research works have also been done in multipath routing to improve the sturdiness of data delivery, to regulate the traffic load, balance the power consumption among nodes, to reduce the end-to-end delay and to improve the network security etc. This routing mechanism provides route resilience irrespective of a fault tolerance and necessary for load balancing and offers QoS. In addition to these benefits, it also includes the reduction in computing time that is needed by the router's CPU, high call acceptance ratio and better security.

The three prerequisites of multipath routing are path discovery, traffic distribution and path maintenance. Path discovery is to determine the accessible paths for a source-destination pair. A protocol can use various criteria to decide either the subset or all possible paths it needs to find out in the discovery process. In the process of traffic distribution, various strategies are followed to allocate traffic over the accessible paths. Path selection algorithm is used to select a subset of available paths according to certain quality of the paths. Hop-count is the traditionally used metric to select the best path. Path maintenance is to regenerate paths after the process of initial path discovery process. This process gets initiated when the path fails. Few multipath protocols have algorithms to frequently monitor and maintain the quality of accessible paths. Many multipath routing protocols have been proposed for various types of networks. Among them, the On-demand routing protocols draws much attention due to its fastness and efficient recovery from the route failures. Protocols such as AODV-BR, AODVM, SMLDR and AOMDV are improve versions of AODV but TORA, PAMOR, ROAM and CHAMP are related to distance vector based routing protocols.

Mobile Adhoc NETwork(MANET) is a collection of self-configuring mobile nodes interconnected by wireless connections. In MANET each node acts as a node as were as routers for forwarding packets. As nodes are mobile, they will frequently change its location and results in high topological configuration. Since there is no centralized coordinator and fixed infrastructure, routing is a complex task and also more vulnerable to security threats. Since it has no predetermined fixed infrastructure, for routing packets each node relies on neighbouring nodes. Routing protocols are essential for data transmission from the source node to the destination node. Such protocols in MANET are available with different characteristics such as routing methodologies and the way preferred to make routing decisions. Protocols may be chosen based on the requirement, but there is no single protocol that solves security related problems. Though MANET is an open medium, providing security is a great challenging issue.

Routing Protocols are mainly classified into three types based on how the routing information is updated. Ad Hoc routing protocols are proactive, reactive and hybrid. Proactive routing protocols (also known as table driven) periodically exchanges the routing information between nodes and it also maintains the network topological information in each node. Reactive routing protocols (also known as on demand) acquire the path when it is required. These protocols will not periodically updates the routing table information and do not maintain the topological information for each node.

Hybrid routing protocols combines the best features of both proactive and reactive routing protocols. Nodes within the transmission range would be communicated using proactive protocols and the nodes outside the transmission range would be communicated using reactive protocols.

The Dynamic Source Routing (DSR) is an on-demand routing protocol to facilitate the notion of source routing and it is competent enough to acquire and hoard multiple routes in a cache to a certain destination. As the new routes are discovered, route caches get updated. Hence route cache plays a vital role in determining whether the route is available to the destination.

3.2.   Security Issues in MANET & WSN

From the past history till the recent development, security is considered to be the most important factor irrespective of any technology. It gains attention in mobile ad hoc networks, since a protected communication must be established between mobile nodes. Certain unique characteristics that cause a number of challenges to security design such as open peer-to-peer network architecture, shared wireless medium, stringent resource constraints, and highly dynamic network topology distinguishes MANETS from other networks. Security is considered to be an important issue in MANETS.

Various attributes that are used to evaluate the security of an ad-hoc network are:

- **Availability:** This service makes sure that the desirable network services are available at the expected time despite of the presence of the attacks. Denial of service, energy starvation attacks and node misbehaviour must be surmounted to achieve high availability.

- **Confidentiality:** Certain information must not be understood by any unauthorized entities. Sensitive information that is transmitted should be encrypted using symmetric or asymmetric encryption techniques.

- **Integrity:** It guarantees that the message sent from one entity to other entity is not modified by any malicious node in the middle of the transmission.

- **Authentication:** This service is used to make certain that the entity communicating with the other entity is a legitimate user. A malicious node could not masquerade as a trusted network node. Through this service, unauthorized access to resource, sensitive information could be prevented.

- **Non-repudiation:** Refers to the ability to make sure that an entity cannot deny the authenticity of their signature on a document or the sending of a message that is originated.

3.2.1. *Vulnerabilities of the Mobile Ad Hoc Networks*

Various vulnerabilities that exist in MANETs are listed as follows:

- **No Central Infrastructure:** These types of networks does not have clear secure boundary and they operate independently of any infrastructure. Hence, deployment of centralized host relationships looks difficult and distributive cooperative scheme works best in this case.

- **Unreliability of Wireless Links:** Attacks on MANET could be from all directions and target on any nodes. There is no clear specification of clear line of defense that is required for every node in order to defend against threats.

- **Multi-hop:** The packets travel from the source node to different mobile nodes before they reach the destination node since this network lacks the facility of central routers and gateways.

- **Dynamic Nature of Topology:** The topology of the MANETs changes frequently. The nodes move continuously that leads to the change in routing information.

- **Device Limitation:** Certain limitations in power, memory and computation power might challenge the users to design a secured protocol that must result in low complexity, memory and computation. Nodes that are attacked flood group of trash messages to make the device to run out of its power. This is considered as DoS (Denial of Service) attack.

3.2.2. Attacks in MANETS

Many attacks exist in the MANET's and they are classified into four types.

- **External Attacks:** These attacks emerge from the outside of the domain. The aim of the attacker is mainly to agitate the nodes from giving the information or to disseminate the fake routing information.
- **Internal Attacks:** The antagonists' steal the valuable information since they reside inside the network and have all access rights.The antagonist acts smart by participating in the network activities either through some malicious impersonation as a new node or it conducts its malicious behaviour by compromising the current node.
- **Passive Attacks:** A passive attack eavesdrops packets and required information is collected by analyzing the packets. This continuous collection of information is used later during the launch of an active attack.
- **Active Attacks:** During this attack, the attacker monitors the communication and takes the control between the two entities and masquerades as one of the entity. These attacks are launched during the active interaction with victims.

3.2.3. Attacks in WSN

Wireless sensor networks are vulnerable to security attacks due to the location of the nodes that are in hostile or hazardous environment, broadcast nature of the transmission medium. Attacks are classified as active and passive attacks. When the data is exchanged in the network without interrupting the communication during an attack, this attack is referred as passive attack. Examples of passive attacks are eavesdropping, traffic analysis, and traffic monitoring.

- **Eavesdropping:** It is termed as the discovery of the communication contents through snooping to the data. This attack comes into action effectively during the communication of the control information about the sensor network configuration.
- **Traffic Analysis:** Communication patterns are analysed during the encrypted message transfer. The information is revealed somehow in an attempt to facilitate an adversary to harm the sensor network.

An active attack is stated as the attack that entails the disruption of the normal functioning of a network that means information modification or fabrication of the information. Examples of active attacks are jamming, impersonating, modification, denial of service (DoS) and message replay.

Routing Attacks in Sensor Networks

Attacks that occur in the network layer are treated as routing attacks. Several attacks that crop up during the routing of messages are:

Spoofing, Altering and Replaying Routing information

Every node acts as a router and the routing information is affected directly.

Selective Forwarding

In this attack, malicious nodes acts as black hole and might refuse to forward packets and those packets are dropped. Hence, the neighbouring nodes come to a conclusion that the node is failed and hence it finds out the alternative routes. The most elusive form of this attack is when an adversary selects the packets for forwarding.

Sinkhole Attack

When a particular node attracts traffic towards it, then it is called as sinkhole attack. The traffic is been attracted through the compromised node from a specific place. The goal of adversary is to make a node as a special attractive compromised node in its surrounding area.

Sybil Attacks

It is defined as the duplication of node in many locations. In other words, it is defined as a malicious node illegitimately appearing in multiple identities.

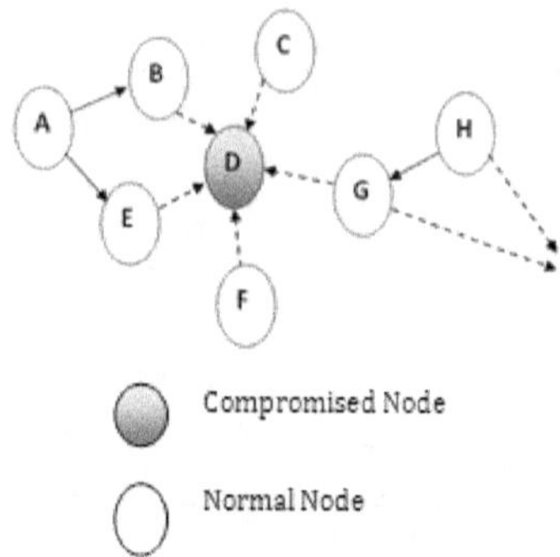

Figure 3.1: Sybil Node that Attack the Normal Nodes

It is also effective against routing algorithms, data aggregation, voting, fair resource allocation and foiling misbehaviour detection. Techniques such as authentication and encryption are used to prevent an adversary to launch this attack on the sensor network.

Wormholes Attacks

Recorded packets are tunnelled from one part of the network to another location, and they are retransmitted. An adversary who resides very close to the base station might disrupt routing with the help of a warm hole.

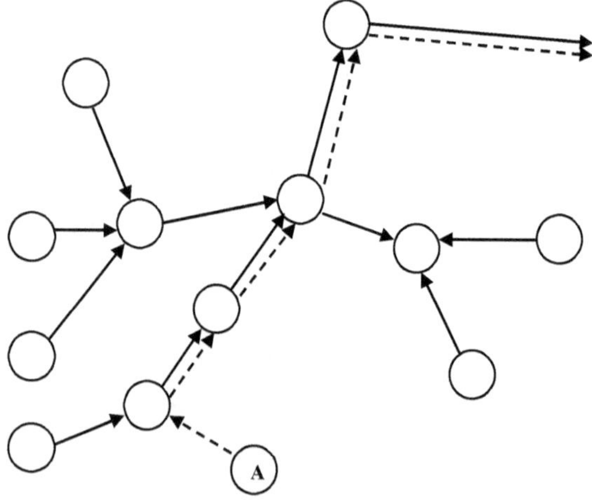

Figure 3.2: Warm Hole Attack in a Network

In other words, wormhole is defined as an out-of-band connection, controlled by the adversary between two physical locations. Here, in this attack the adversary installs the radio transceivers at both ends of the wormhole. In this attack the adversary creates an illusion that the locations are directly connected even though they are located away from the base station. It is very hard to detect as the communication medium is not clear between the two bad nodes. The hop count is controlled and verified which limits the self-organizing criteria of an ad-hoc network.

HELLO Flood Attacks

Many protocols require nodes to broadcast HELLO PACKETS to give an idea about their presence to the neighbour nodes. Receiving nodes create an assumption that the nodes are within the RF range of the sender. This assumption is considered as a false assumption when an attacker transmits routing information with a high transmission range to confirm that every node in the network that the neighbour node is malicious. As a result of this, while sending the information to the base station, the victim nodes try to go through the attacker as they know that it is their neighbour and are ultimately spoofed by the attacker. Security in wireless sensor networks could be classified into four main categories. They are a) obstacles to sensor network security, b) the requirements of a secure wireless sensor network c) attacks and defensive measures.

Obstacles to Sensor Network Security: Wireless sensor network is a special network that has many constraints. The constraints could be identified under obstacles to sensor networks are:

- Very limited resources
- Unreliable communication
- Unattended operation

Very Limited Resources: Certain security approaches require memory space and storage area for implementation.

Unreliable Communication: A secured network requires a defined protocol to ensure proper communication. Certain features that give space for unreliable communication are:

1. **Unreliable Transfer:** Packets might be damaged due to errors that occur in channel or it might be dropped due to the congestion of nodes. The unreliable wireless communication channel might also lead to packets loss or packets missing. Due to this high error rate, more resources are required to handle the error. If the protocol that

doed not defines proper error handling measures then, this leads to lose of critical security packets.

2. **Conflicts:** Due to the unreliable channel, communication also becomes unreliable. Conflicts might arise in the middle of packets transferring and therefore it leads to failure of transfer.

3. **Latency:** Latency occurs due to multi-hop routing, network congestion and node processing.

Unattended Operation: Sensor networks may be left unattended for long periods of time. Three main caveats to unattended sensor nodes are listed as follows.

- **Exposure to Physical Attacks:** Sensors deployed in an environment are open to antagonists', bad weather etc. Hence physical attacks to those sensors are high when compared to a PC that is in a secure place.

- **Managed Remotely:** It is highly difficult to detect physical tampering due to the remote management of a sensor network. For example when a sensor network is deployed to manage remote exploration of an area to gather military information of an opponent, the node might not have any physical contact with the forces that has to make contact.

- **No Central Management Point:** The distributive nature of the network increases the vitality of the network. Incorrect design might lead to inefficiency and fragile nature.

3.3.   Security Requirements

Security encompasses the features of data confidentiality, data integrity, data freshness, availability, self organization, time synchronization, secure localization and authentication.

- **Data Freshness:** It identifies that the data is new or current and it also ensures that no old messages have been replayed. This feature plays a vital role in sharing key strategy. New keys are generated for sharing takes time for propagation over the entire network. In this case, it is simple for an adversary to do the replay attack. The sensor does not know the new key change time. Hence it becomes easy to break off the normal work of a sensor.

- **Self Organizing:** The main important feature of the wireless sensor network is independent and flexible enough to be self-healed and organized based upon the situations. Due to the dynamism in its infrastructure, it becomes a great challenge to wireless sensor networks. An efficient technique is required for distributing the public key, multi-hop routing, and key management and to build the trust relation among sensors. Lack of self organizing feature leads to damage that originates from an attack or even to the devastation of perilous environment.

- **Time Synchronization:** Some form of time synchronization is followed in many sensor network applications. End-to-end delay of a packet is computed when a packet travels from one sensor to another sensor. Group synchronization is the factor that is required by a collaborative sensor network.

- **Secure Localization:** The effectiveness of a sensor network mainly rely on its ability to locate exactly and correctly the position of each sensor in the network. Faults could be identified easily with the help of the accurate information location. An attacker can easily change the location information by reporting false signal strengths and replaying signals.

3.4.   Role of Multipath Routing in Security aspects

Routing protocols maintains routing tables to store the information about the next hop towards the destination node. It maintains a caching mechanism to store the information. Multipath routing is an alternative routing technique that selects multiple paths for delivering the data from source to destination. This type of routing uses redundant paths and it addresses issues such as reliability, security and load balancing issues that occurred during single path routing. Various benefits of multipath routing are:

- Reliability and fault tolerance
- Load Balancing
- QoS Improvement
- Reduced delay
- Bandwidth Aggregation

This routing improves security because of the nature of multiple paths. When data is transferred from multiple paths, even in the presence of malicious paths, the original data is obtained at the receiving end through the reliable paths. Through this multipath routing, the malicious attacks could be measured by increasing the confidentiality and robustness of transmitted data. The coding technique is incorporated with multipath routing and data is encoded before transmission and it is decoded only at the destination node. Many protocols are based on the popular on-demand routing protocols, DSR and AODV. The summary of protocols based on few factors is listed as shown in table 3.1.

Table 3.1: Summary of Protocols

Protocols	SMR (Split Multipath Routing)	MP-DSR (Multipath-Dynamic Source Routing)	AODMV (Adhoc on-demand Multi-Distance Vector)
Source or Distance vector routing.	Source	Source	DV
Route discovery	Shortest delay path and it is maximally disjoint route.	Set of maximally disjoint paths that satisfy QoS requirement.	link- or node disjoint paths.
Traffic distribution	Concurrently there are two paths.	Paths are not specified.	Single path.
Route Maintenance	New discovery is immediately attempted. Maintained only when both paths fail.	All paths broken QoS is no longer satisfied.	when last path fails.

3.5. Broadcasting

Mobile ad hoc networks (MANETs) are self-organizing and the constituent mobile nodes communicate with each other as autonomous hosts in the absence of a fixed infrastructure. Recently, MANETs are deployed to places where the network is required to be promptly established such as military operations and disaster relief. However, the mobile nodes merely operate with limited resources such as processing, communication, and energy. The nodes further have the characteristic of high mobility. Thus, MANET has the properties of frequently route breakage and unpredictable topology changes.

Clearly, these properties make the transmission methods widely used in fixed infrastructures inappropriate for MANET. Broadcasting is an alternative which is a one-to-all transmission method, namely a packet or a message generated by a node, called the source, is sent to all other nodes in the network. Moreover, broadcasting is an important operation in applications performing route discovery (Johnson&Maltz, 1996; Park&Corson, 1997; Pearlman & Haas, 1999; Perkins &Royer, 1999), updating the network knowledge, or sending an alarm signal. However, it seems greedy and excessive in aspect of resource limitation, especially energy which is a major concern in MANET, since the nodes transmit packets in a multi-hop communication manner. Therefore, the energy cost of broadcast packet transmission (i.e., the number of transmissions) should be minimized to conserve the energy of the mobile nodes.

Blind flooding is the most straightforward approach to broadcasting. Specifically, every node in the network forwards the broadcast packet exactly once. It ensures the full coverage of the entire network: all the nodes in the network are guaranteed to receive the broadcast packet in case that the network is static and the occurrence of collision and error is not considered during propagation. However, flooding may generate excessive redundant transmissions which cause a critical problem, referred to as the broadcast storm problem (Ni et al., 1999), introducing communication contention and collision due to sharing wireless resources and overlapping coverage areas among nodes.

The broadcast storm problem can be readily avoided by reducing the number of retransmissions. In order to alleviate the broadcast storm problem, probability-based, area based, and neighbour knowledge approaches control the amount of traffic, that is, each node determines whether or not to retransmit the broadcast packet.

The probability-based approach controls message flood with a predefined probability or received packet count. Obviously, it resembles blind flooding when the probability that a node retransmits the broadcast packet equals to one. In the area-based approach, each node determines whether or not to rebroadcast the packet with evaluation of its additional coverage area by rebroadcasting. If the additional coverage is less than the threshold, the node abandons retransmitting. This method relies on location or distance information of nodes to determine rebroadcasting. The neighbour knowledge approach utilizes one or two hop neighbour information obtained via periodical hello packets to reduce redundant rebroadcasting. This approach allows retransmitting only when it results in any additional neighbour to be reached.

According to the methods controlling message flood, network overhead can be significantly reduced. However, some problems can occur such as end-to-end delay or latency and unreliability. Each node requires a certain waiting time to examine whether or not to rebroadcast a packet. In the area-based approach, for example, a node sets a random waiting time when a previously unseen packet arrives and it observes the duplicate packet arriving during the waiting time. Since nodes hold a packet for waiting times, the time spent on propagation from the packet origination to reach a node, namely end-to-end delay, increases.

Reliability is considered in a network that nodes are fully connected to others in a single or multi-hop fashion and the network is static. When a node determines to discard a packet with an examination of the necessity of rebroadcasting, some one-hop neighbours may not receive the packet. Furthermore, the packet is unreachable to nodes which have the sole connection through the neighbours.

More precisely, a perfectly reliable broadcasting with minimizing redundancy is defined as a problem finding the minimum connected dominating set (MCDS) where a connected dominating set states that each node either belongs to the set or has a neighbour which belong to the set and is fully connected to others. Unfortunately, the problem of finding the MCDS is classified as NP-complete even if the global topology information is given (Lim & Kim, 2001; Lou & Wu, 2002).

Some broadcasting schemes form a conjunction of area-based and neighbour knowledge approaches, called hybrid broadcasting schemes, to efficiently resolve redundant transmission, unreliability, and latency. Based on that outer nodes from the sender are prone to have more additional coverage than inner nodes (i.e., area-based approach), the outer takes higher priority of retransmission than the inner: when a node receives a previously unseen packet, it first sets a waiting time determined in inverse proportion to the distance to the sender. Instead of computation of additional coverage to make a determination of packet drop, each node examines whether all its neighbours receive the packet (i.e., neighbour knowledge) to resolve a potential unreliability.

3.5.1. Issues in Broadcasting

The Broadcast Storm

As mentioned above, flooding is the simplest solution to broadcasting. The fundamental idea behind flooding is that every node participates in transmission of a packet exactly once to deliver it throughout the network in a multi-hop fashion. Hence, intermediate nodes have the obligation to retransmit the packet. This leads to n transmissions in a network of n hosts for a single packet. It achieves perfectly reliable broadcasting if the communication channel is error-free with no collision.

Unfortunately, redundancy, contention, and collision can be observed which are referred to as the broadcast storm problem in (Ni et al., 1999). The main reason for redundancy is that the coverage of a node may overlap with others nearly placed. In other words, several intermediate nodes perform redundant transmission in case that all neighbours within the transmission range of the node have already received the packet. Additionally, because of the lack of bandwidth, wireless resource sharing, and the absence of collision detection, redundant transmissions are prone to trigger noticeable contention and collision.

The broadcast storm problem seriously worsens if the size of the network increases and nodes are densely distributed. Figure1 illustrates a network with five nodes. When a broadcast packet is generated and forwarded by source A, the packet reaches to all the nodes by node B as shown in figure 1(b). Figures 1(c) and 1(d) illustrates redundant broadcasting by nodes C, D, and E. In addition to the redundancy in figure 1(c), the hidden node problem can be found in the network based on contention-based protocols including ALOHA (Abramson, 1970), slotted ALOHA (Saadawi & Ephremides, 1981), CSMA (carrier sense multiple access) and IEEE 802.11.

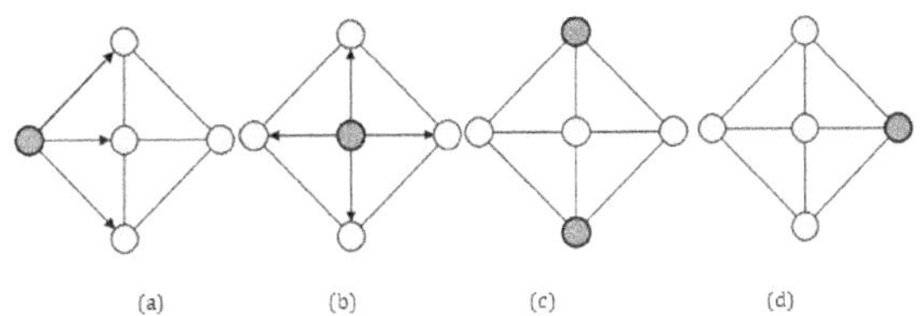

Figure 3.3: A Sample Network with Five nodes: (a) Broadcasting by Source A (b) Optimal Broadcasting (c) Redundant Broadcasting and Hidden Node Problem without RTS/CTS Handshake (d) Redundant Broadcasting

Unreliability and Latency

Apparently, packet drop becomes an essential function in broadcasting to reduce the broadcast redundancy, which is implicit in resource usage, by judging necessity of transmission. The packet drop effectively resolves the broadcast storm problem and even reduces resource usage. Unfortunately, end-to-end unreliability and latency can arise due to packet drop by an incorrect judgement.

Because of the properties of MANET, flooding rarely guarantees perfect reliability. For instance, some nodes are often isolated from the network. In spite of difficulties, a perfectly reliable broadcasting is necessary in some applications (e.g., the localization in (Doherty et al., 2001; Niculescu & Nath, 2001; Shang & Ruml, 2004)). The underlying assumption here is that the network is seen as static or a snapshot of mobile networks with the error-free channel. In this network, flooding ensures the perfectly reliable delivery. However, some nodes in the network may not receive the packet when flooding is implemented with packet flood control. As far as a node on standby for transmission determines the necessity of transmission without global topology information or local announcements representing packet reception from its neighbours, the node is prone to make a poor determination. In general, packet loss occurs by collision and it results in poor reliability as well.

Latency is also introduced from the packet drop which is the time spent from when a packet is originated until it reaches to a node. Each node waits for a certain time to make a determination of retransmission in packet flood control. It is primarily required for appropriate flood control. Furthermore, packet drop is likely to block the shortest path of a packet in sparse networks. In other words, the packet makes a detour to nodes in specific regions.

Typically, many researches aim at minimizing the number of transmission while attempting to ensure the full coverage of the network at the same time. Recently, since end-to-end delay becomes a major issue in designing networks, rapid spread of a broadcast packet is indeed considered as well.

3.5.2. *Broadcasting in MANET*

The broadcasting methods can be classified as blind flooding, probability-based, area-based, and neighbour knowledge approaches (Williams & Camp, 2002).

Blind flooding (Ho et al., 1999; Jetcheva et al., 2001) requires each node to rebroadcast a broadcast packet to all its neighbors and this continues until all nodes retransmit the packet at least once. In order to alleviate the inefficiencies of blind flooding, probability-based methods assign a probability to a node to determine whether or not to rebroadcast. Area based methods allow a node to rebroadcast a packet if its transmission range sufficiently covers additional area. Neighbour knowledge methods decide the retransmission of the packet based on local neighbour lists through hello packets. A performance comparison of some of the schemes can be found in (Williams & Camp, 2002).

3.6. Route Discovery and Route Maintenance

Dynamic Source Routing protocol (DSR) is an efficient routing protocol designed for using in multi-hop wireless ad hoc networks. It is suitable for the network which is entirely self organizing and self configuring nodes without any fixed infrastructure or centralized coordinator. It involves two steps to accomplish a task such as route discovery and route maintenance. It supports high rate of mobility.

Dynamic Source Routing is an on-demand routing protocol, which initiates route discovery if mobile node has a packet to transmit based on source routing. The route for data transmission is specified in the packet header to reach its destination. The intermediate node checks for the route specified in packet header, decides whether to accept the packet or to forward it to the next node. If the destination address matches with its own address, the received packet is successfully delivered otherwise forwarded to the upstream neighbour node.

Routing table cache records the possible routes from the source node to the destination node. The node and its neighbour are persistently updating its cache for the fresh route. If a node tries to find a path for packet transmission, it checks for the destination address is its neighbour's address or it is available in its route cache. If path is known, the preferred route is entered in the packet header for transmission. Otherwise, the source node initiates the route discovery process for discovering a route.

The chosen path should be monitored continuously to check all the communicating nodes are in the same transmission range. If the communicating nodes moved out of the transmission range, the packet will not be properly destined to the intended recipient.

Route maintenance is the challenging task to identify the link failure and to monitor the transmitted packets is properly reaching the destination. If the link failure is identified, then it should be intimated to the source node with route error message.

Route Cache

Based on DSR protocol procedure, participating nodes routing information are stored in a route cache. Each node will have its own Route Cache. The information available in the Route Cache is added by listening the attached links between nodes. If link is broken then the entry about the particular node should be removed from the cache.

Route Cache has some of the operations like Insert(), Get() and Delete(). Information learned from the source route should be updated in the route cache. The source route from the sending node to the destination node is available; it could be retrieved using GET function.

If a route in the cache is unidirectional this means that another communicating node is not reachable or not available. Since the entry can be removed from the route cache table.

3.7. Summary

This chapter discuss about different challenges and attacks in MANETs and WSN environments. The security features and its possible classification are discussed. The role of multipath routing in MASNET environment in association with security features has also been briefed. The last part of this chapter discuss about the route discovery and route maintenance concepts. The main objective of this work is to evaluate the impact of broadcasting in scheme in the MASNET environment. The subsequent chapter discuss about SeMuRAMAS and multipoint relay based Dynamic MPR routing scheme.

CHAPTER 4

DYNAMIC MULTIPATH ROUTING SCHEME

As discussed in the previous chapter, multipath routing algorithms are generally suggested to overcome the nodes and link failures. Security integration in a multipath routing algorithm prevents   node misbehaviour and routing attacks. This research work is primarily considering the role of broadcasting sequences in a secured multipath routing algorithm. The SeMuRAMAS algorithm has been used for comparing the effectiveness of newly proposed algorithms.

4.1.   Introduction to SeMuRAMAS

The Secure multipath routing algorithm for mobile ad hoc and sensor networks (SeMuRAMAS) is an extension of Dynamic Source Routing algorithm. The DSR is a reactive routing approach which is widely used as a basis for a large set of extended routing protocols. The SeMuRAMAS algorithm mainly contains two phases, route discovery and route maintenance. These two phases are essential to establish and maintain route between source and destination nodes. Especially in the context of wireless sensor networks, destination node represents the base station.

The route discovery phase primarily establishes a set of possible paths to destination node. The Path-disjointness threshold value is required to compute the minimal number of shared nodes. The route discovery phase uses six datagrams known as route request datagram, route response datagram, notification datagram, list forwarding datagram, rout error datagram and threshold tuning datagram.

The route maintenance phase is a mechanism used by the intermediate nodes when the route failure occurs or change in network topology to construct the new path. Watchdog mechanism is used in this phase to detect the identities of misbehaving nodes. The route maintenance phase will be able to quickly reconstruct the path using data available in the intermediate node caches. A path can fail due to collision and/or nodes mobility. It is essential to recover broken paths immediately to ensure the reliability of data. After route establishment and during data forwarding, when a node in an established route fails to send the packet to the next hop or detects that a neighbour is not forwarding the datagram, SeMuRAMAS considers the route as broken and sends a Route Error RErr to the source node to inform it about the identity of the unavailable node. This mechanism is strengthened by applying a watchdog mechanism.

4.2.   Security Mechanism in SeMuRAMAS

In Mobile Ad-hoc networks (MANETs), the mobile devices use a radio channel to send information to another mobile device/node. Due to the nature of MANETs malicious nodes can eavesdrop the packets, tunnel them to another location in the network and retransmit them. This generates a false scenario that the original sender is in the neighborhood of the remote location. The tunneling procedure forms a wormhole and it is conducted by collusive attackers. If a fast transmission path exists between the two ends of the wormhole, the tunneled packets can propagate faster than those through normal multi-hop route. Intrusion Detection Systems (IDS) have been adopted as the second line of defense to protect ad hoc networks. The Watchdog is the first snooping intrusion detection protocol for MANETs and it is basically relies upon DSR protocol. In this case, each node participates by watching its downstream node on the route from source to destination for ensuring the packet without modification.

Weichao Wang et al(2006) state that wormhole attack is classified into three groups known as closed group, half open group and open group according to the format of the tunnel and attacker's capability.

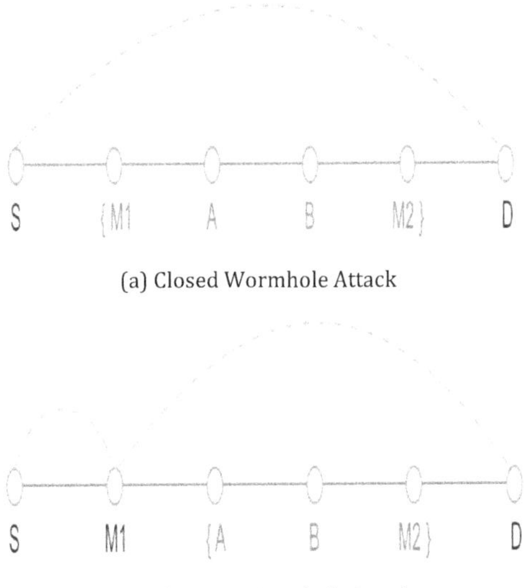

(a) Closed Wormhole Attack

(b) Half-open Wormhole Attack

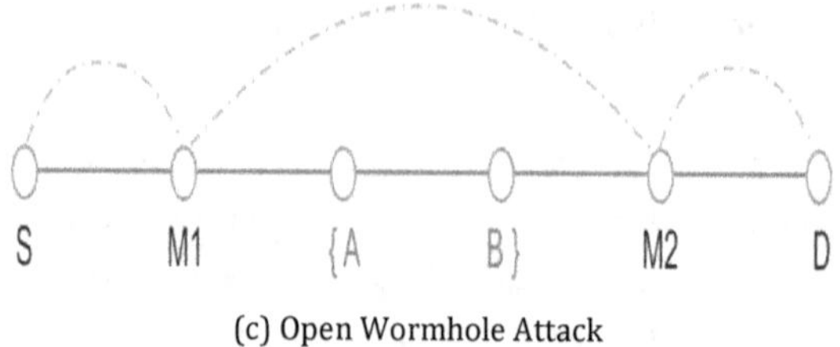

(c) Open Wormhole Attack

Figure 4.1: Types of Wormhole Attacks

———— Physical Link,   - - - - False Route, { } Wormhole

Figure 4.1 depicts the type of wormhole attacks. In this, M1 and M2 are malicious nodes, S is the source node, D represents destination node and A, B are normal mobile nodes. The nodes between the curly-braces "{ }" are wormhole attacks, which are on the path but it is invisible to S and D. In Figure 4.1a, M1 and M2 tunnel the neighbor discovery beacons from S to D and vice-versa, so S and D think that they are direct neighbors. Both M1 and M2 are in the wormhole. In Figure 4.1b, M1 is a neighbor of S and it tunnels its beacons through M2 to D. Only one malicious node is visible to S and D. In an open wormhole, both attackers are visible to S and D as shown in Figure 4.1c.

The Watchdog technique is used to withstand the several types of routing attacks such as wormhole attack, etc and the deployed digital signature algorithm protects the integrity of the datagram's that are exchanged during the process and thus it prevents attackers from counterfeiting routes. Certain nodes that uses watchdog mechanism determines the status of the corresponding neighbor nodes that is responsible for forwarding the datagram whether they receive or not. In addition to the detection of misbehaving nodes, this mechanism is used to detect route errors and if the route is broken, it generates the error message.

The watchdog mechanism is used to detect the nodes that misbehave in a network. The following figure 4.2 illustrates the mechanism of watchdog.

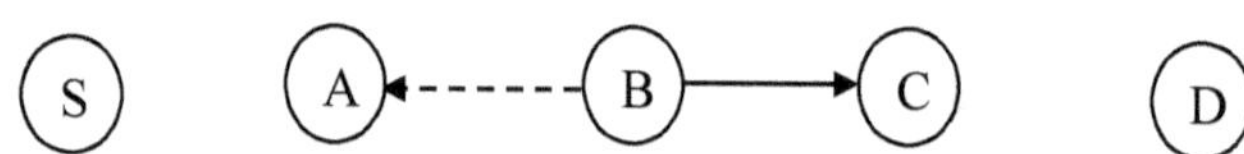

Figure 4.2 a: Path Exist from S to D through A,B,C

For Example, Figure 4.1aassume there exists a path from node S to D through intermediate nodes A,B and C. Node A could not transmit to node C, but it listens on node B'S TRAFFIC. When A transmits a packet to B to forward to C, A can tell the status of the transmission of B , whether it has been tampered with the payload or the header.

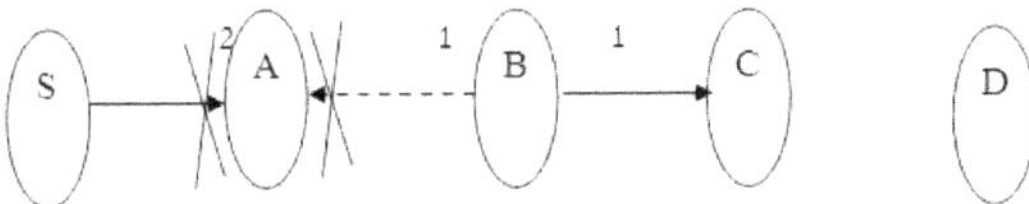

Figure 4.2 b: Node A does not Hear B Forward Packet 1 to C, because B's Transmission Collides at A with Packet 2 from the Source S

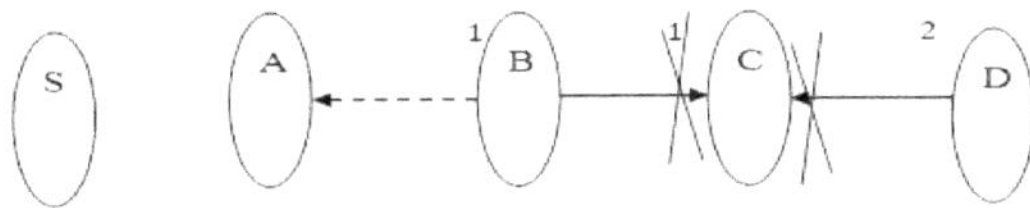

Figure 4.2 c: Node A believes that B has Forwarded Packet 1 on to C, though C Never Received the Packet Due to a Collision with Packet 2

The watchdog mechanism is implemented by keeping the details of recently sent packets in a buffer in order to compare each overhead packet with the packet present in the buffer for a match. If it is same, the packet is removed from the buffer because it is already forwarded. The watchdog increases the failure tally that is responsible for forwarding the packet when the packet remains in the buffer for a period longer than a certain timeout. If the tally exceeds a certain threshold bandwidth, the misbehaving node is determined and the source gets the notification message about it. Using this mechanism, the replay attacks are detected to some extent. To detect replay attacks, much maintenance is required to store the state information at each node since it examines its neighbors in order to make sure that retransmission of a packet is not done. Detecting replay attacks would be neither efficient nor an effective use of the watchdog mechanism.

According to Bayrem Triki et al., 2012, in order to secure routing algorithm against set of attacks the security mechanism has to ensure three main properties. First, node should be able to authenticate each others during the process of routes establishment. Datagrams generated with forged information should be discarded before reaching the destination mobile node. Second, every node should not only be in charge of generating and forwarding datagrams to destination node, but also of controlling the behavior of its neighbors. In this context, the watchdog technique is used to detect nodes that do not forward the datagrams as expected.

A node which uses the watchdog technique is able to determine whether its neighbor nodes are forwarding the datagram they receive or not. If the packet is not forwarded within a certain period, this neighbor is considered as malicious (Lee, 2007). Every node should maintain two lists: a list of one-hop neighbors and a list of two hop neighbors. The two lists are created by letting every node periodically perform a two-hop broadcast of a Hello Message (i.e., by setting the TTL equal to 2). A node, say *n1* which receives a generated Hello message by a node, say *n0*, with a TTL equal to 2, appends the identity of *n0* to its list of neighbors, appends it own identity (i.e., *n1*), decreases by one the TTL, and forwards the packet. A node, say *n2*, which receives a datagram with a TTL equal to 1 from the neighbor node *n1*, appends the identity of the sender (i.e., *n0*) to its list of two hop neighbors, and marks this node as being reachable through the immediate sender *n1*. Third, when a node detects a malicious neighbor, both the source and the destination nodes should be informed.

To protect the routing algorithm against forgery of false routing information, we use a signature scheme to authenticate nodes and guarantee the integrity of the information they exchange. We suppose that, in the case of WSN, every node joining the network is authenticated by the BS. Intermediate verification of packets signature allows discarding compromised packets before they reach the destination nodes, which optimizes the used energy and communication resources, and reduces the overhead of the signature verification process performed by the destination node.

During the routes establishment, every node which generates or forwards the RReq, appends its identity, the identity of the next receiving nodes, and sur-signs the route record. A node receiving the forwarded message verifies whether the last appended signature is correct, checks if it is the presumed destination, determines the immediate sender (the neighbor node from which the packet is being forwarded) of that datagram and makes sure that it is a neighbor. If it is the case, it appends its identity, the identity of the possible next hops and sur-signs the datagram. In the context of WSN, signature is performed using the elliptic threshold signature algorithm provided by Sliti, 2008 is used. It allows to generate for a public key kpub, n associated secret keys kpr1,....., kprn. Every signature created using one of the private keys, say kpri, can be checked using kpub. Every node uses its own private key for signature, while the same public key is used by all the other nodes for the purpose of signature verification. In the context of general types of Adhoc networks, where nodes can enter and leave the network at any time perfid, and no resource limitations exist, regular signature can be used. Every node should have its own private and public keys, where a certificate, containing this public key, is delivered by a certification authority.

Mobiles nodes will use the certificates of the senders to check the integrity of the signed datagrams. We assume that each mobile node has the ability to contact a certification authority repository to download the certificate of any node in the network. These techniques increase the resilience to nodes compromise, especially in the context of WSN they protect against nodes capture. The protection is done by: (a) using digital signature to authenticate packet content and discarding invalid datagrams (b) using the identification of captured node based on applied watchdog mechanism and intermediate signature; and (c) authorizing x shared nodes in order to be tolerant to the discard of compromised paths involving captured node, which assures that, even when part of the nodes have been captured, the rest of the network remains secure.

In the context of WSN, where threshold signature is used, if a node is duplicated, and its key is used by a malicious node, MD will notice the attack by detecting that the same key was used by several nodes. To do so, MD checks whether two nodes having the same identities have participated in forwarding the RReq. If it is not the case, for each signature appended to the RReq, the MD determines the identity of the signer node, and verifies whether it could really produce this signature if its private key was used (in the case of WSNs the MD, which is the base station, is assumed to know all the mobile nodes private keys). Note that the use of the public key is not sufficient to authenticate the nodes, because it does not allow detecting whether the same private key was used several times to generate the sur-signed RReq. When the BS detects that a node has used the private key of another node, or a node has participated several times in the same RReq, it forwards an alert containing the identity of the compromised nodes, asking the remaining nodes in the network to reject any packet sent from that node in the future. When a node receives a second copy of the RReq, it signs and stores the received path in the RP list, where each identity, in the received path, is signed by intermediate nodes. If a malicious node wants to modify the RP list, it must use the signatures of all nodes involved in the modified path to re-sign each identity which is impossible. In addition, when an intermediate node eliminates a received RP list instead of forwarding it, the watchdog mechanism used by neighbor nodes will detect such behavior.

SeMuRAMAS is also protected against a set of routing attacks such as the wormhole attack (Triki, 2009), where a malicious node receives packets, tunnels them to another location in the network, and re-send them. In the case of an out-of-band channel establishment, a malicious node may collude with another node, which is typically located near destination node, to make the routing paths that go over them, look shorter (in terms of number of hops) than expected. Such behavior could compromise the discovery k–x-connected paths.

Using the watchdog mechanism and intermediate signature, the wormhole attack will be detected. In fact, a malicious node could forward a packet to non neighbor node using a high powered transmission. Since the node should append its identity and the identity of immediate receivers to the route record and sur-sign them, two situations could happen: (a) If the malicious node, specifies a correct identity of the immediate receiver, the watchdog neighbors, verify the signature in the datagram and detect that the packet was forwarded to a non neighbor node. When the malicious datagram is forwarded to destination node, together with the alert generated by the watchdog nodes, the latter could use the signature as an evidence to prove the identity of the malicious node; or (b) the malicious node specifies the identity of a neighbor node when it signs the route record, but forwards the datagram to a non neighbor node. In that case, the neighbor nodes will detect that the node has appended an identity of a non neighbor node, which will receive the packet. The watchdog nodes will broadcast an alert, containing the identity of the malicious node, asking the remaining nodes in the network to reject any datagram sent from that node in the future.

4.3.   K-X Connectivity

The source node A needs to establish three $(k = 3)$ routes to the destination mobile node (MD) sharing at maximum two nodes between them $(x = 2)$. In SeMuRAMAS, it is hard to respect three disjoint paths without tuning the threshold x. A generates and broadcasts a $RReq$ with a disjointness threshold x equal to 2. In the Figure 4.2, nodes are represented by circles, and an edge connects two nodes if they are able to directly communicate together. The RP lists stored by each node are represented by rectangles. Node B receives the first packet directly from A and receives a second copy though two other paths which are $< A, C, B >$ and $< A, C, E, B >$. As each time node B drops a duplicated packet, it stores the routing path used by this copy in its RP list, the routing path RP will be equal to $<< A, C, B >< A, C, E, B >>$. The $RReq$ is forwarded to neighbor nodes until it reaches MD on the shortest path $Rsp = < A, B, D, F, MD >$.

As shown in Figure 4.3, based on the number of minimum common nodes RCN which is set to 2 in the Notification Packet (ND), the RP lists are only sent by nodes F, M, D and E. In fact, at the response step, when Node F receives the ND from MD, it decreases the value of remaining number of common nodes (RCN) to 1 and forwards this packet to its neighbors. This node applies the filter $F1$ on its RP list based on the content of the $RPBS$ list received for the destination node. Note that this $RPBS$ contains the two following paths $< A,B,D, F,MD >$ and $< A,B,D,E,M,MD>$. Using the filter $F1$, paths $< A,B,E, F >$ and $< A,B,E,M, F >$, in the RP list of the node F, will be eliminated because they have more than $RCN -1 = 1$ shared node with the $RPBS$.

As the *RP* list of node *F* is empty, its *RP* list will be sent back to the source node. When node *M* receives the *NP* from *MD*, it decreases *RCN* o 1 and applies the two filters *F1* and *F2* on its *RP* list. By applying *F1*, node *M*, will discard the path< *ABDFM* >from its *RP* list, because it has more than *RCN* – 1 = 1 shared nodes with the first path < *A,B,D, F,MD* >of the *RPBS* list. When the node *M* receives a second copy of *ND* from the node *F* it will discard it.

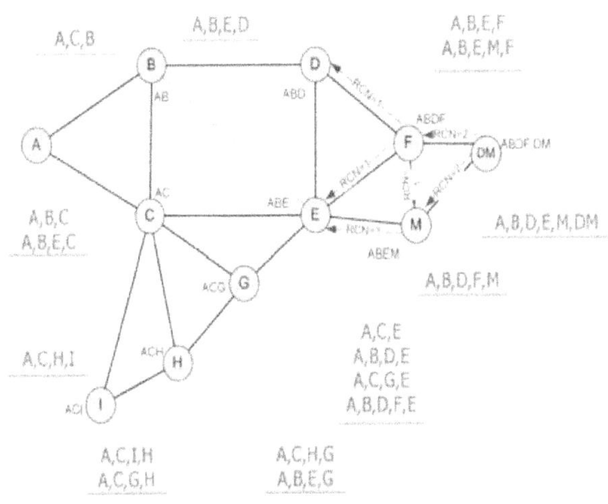

Figure 4.3: SeMuRAMAS Response Process

When nodes *D* and *E* receive *ND* from node *F*, they decrease the value of *RCN* to 0. By applying the two filters *F1* and *F2*, nodeD will not send the path< *A,B,E,D* >stored in its RP list. In fact, the use of filter F1 lets nodeE keep only paths < A, C,E > and < A, C,G,E > in its RP list. However, < A, C,E > and < A, C,G,E > share node C and node E accepts only RCN – 1 = 0 common nodes. Therefore, when it applies the filter F2, node E is forced to keep only the shortest path it knows, which is < A, C,E >. When the node E receives a second copy of the ND from the node M, it discards it. When the neighbors of nodes D and E receive the NP with an RCN set to 0, they discard this packet without sending any information. At the end, the source node A, has a list of paths available to MD which is equal to Lp = {< A, C, E>}. The RPBS, which is extracted from the route response datagram (RRep), together with the list of paths Lp will be used to determine the set of routes, characterized by k = 3 and x = 2, to MD. By applying the reconstruction algorithm described in Subsection 3.3, the final list of reconstructed paths Lcp will be equal to: Lcp = {< A, C,E, F,BS >< A,B,D, F,BS ><A, B,E,M,BS >}.

4.3.1. *Multipath Algorithm based on K-X Connectivity*

Certain requirements have to be accomplished by a multipath routing algorithm based on the notion of k-x connectivity.

- The SeMuRAMS algorithm should be functioning properly in both Adhoc and Sensor networks by considering the constraints such as available computational resources, battery energy available on nodes and security of the area in which the network is deployed.

- The algorithm must withstand to attacks. In addition, it must check whether the packets are forwarded properly in the networks and the intermediate nodes' identities are updated to the routing requests.

- The identities and behavior nodes that are engrossed during the multiple routes establishment must be evidenced. These evidences are referred during the digital investigation of trace backing a unocccured attack, locating the malicious nodes and in proving the existence of fake routes.

- Algorithm must be a reactive one.

- This algorithm must be distributed where the intermediate nodes starts the process of gathering the information about the potential available paths as soon as the route request datagrams is posted. It is necessary to share the route computation tasks in the view point of WSN. The main advantage is to withstand the failure in the case of attacks.

- The network performance must be preserved.

- When the source node fails in locating set of paths with the specified threshold value, then the algorithm must provide a facility to indicate the minimal disjointness value supported by the current network topology.

4.4. Common Issues in SeMuRAMAS

In this research, SeMuRAMAS algorithm is considered for comparison with the proposed algorithm, since the existing and proposed methods consider security and multipath routing in MASNETs. The following are the list of issues observed in SeMuRAMAS.

- When a mobile node joins the network, it broadcasts a two hop HELLO message. Therefore each node is required to maintain two up-to-date lists. The first list denotes the list of neighbours and the second one denotes the neighbours of each neighbour.

- The disjointness threshold is set by the sender to specify the maximum number of nodes that could be shared by any two paths among the set of paths to establish with the destination node.
- Broadcasts the RREQ to all nodes in the networks and insists to store the information regardless of possible routes between source and destination.
- In SeMuRAMAS the network overload will increase depending up on the number of nodes and the value of the threshold x.In majority of the situations the increase of overhead is unavoidable.
- High number of lists of paths may be generated which it influences to increase the number of datagrams.

4.5. Multipoint Relay

Broadcast traffic is often used to disseminate information to all nodes.

Another important use of broadcast is to find unicast routes in ad hoc networks. Because all nodes will be required to receive or to retransmit, hence all nodes will have resources consumed, thus broadcast efficiency is very important. Due to the potentially dynamic nature of ad hoc networks, Multipoint Relay algorithms are much more robust and effective in-terms of overhead.

In MASNETs, packets can be forwarded on the same interface that it arrived on. Instead of pure flooding where all nodes retransmit all packets, with Multipoint Relays (MPR) packets are forwarded only by the node's MPRs in order to reduce the number of transmissions that are needed to successfully deliver the packets.

A MPR set is a subset of a node's one-hop neighbours, such that together these subsets are able to reach all the two-hop neighbours. In order to calculate the MPR set, the node must have link state information about all one-hop and two-hop neighbors.

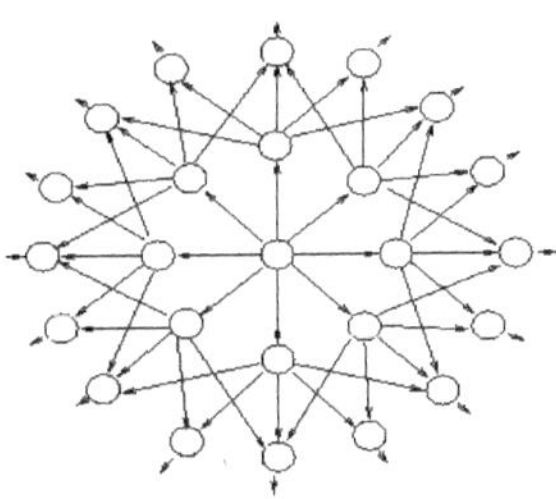

Figure 4.4: Flooding a Packet in a Wireless Multi-hop Network

The objective of the Multipoint relay is to reduce the number of duplicate retransmissions during the process of forwarding a broadcast packet. This technique is used to restrict the set of nodes that retransmits a packet from all nodes, to a subset of all nodes. The size of the subset mainly depends on the network topology. The below fig 4.4 shows the process of flooding a packet in a wireless multi-hop network. The arrows in the Fig 4.4 illustrates the way, information is passed.

Figure 4.5 illustrates the usage of Multipoint relays that are denoted by black circle. MPRs are used to flood a packet in a wireless multihop network from the centre node. The arrow indicates the path, information is passed. Flooding is achieved by selecting neighbours as Multipoint relays (MPRs). Every node has the capability of computing its own group of MPRs as a subset of its symmetric neighbor nodes chosen so that all 2 hop neighbors could be reached through a MPR. It means that a symmetric link exist between the local node and MPR.

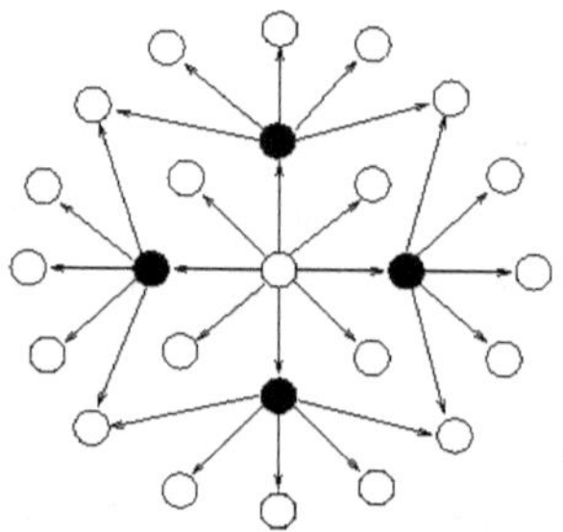

Figure 4.5: Flooding a Packet Network from the Centre Node

For example, by considering the scenario shown in the fig 4.6, node A selects the black nodes as MPRs. This way all two hop nodes could be reached through a MPR. Node B will not retransmit traffic from A that is to be flooded.

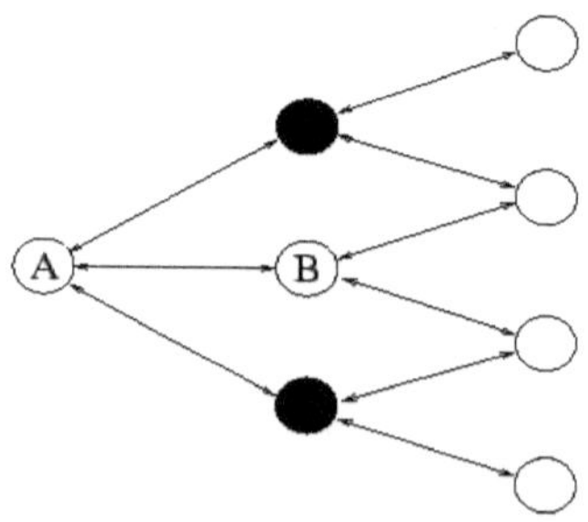

Figure 4.6: Node A has Selected the Black Nodes as its MPRs

Multipath routing protocols that has been proposed for Ad hoc network based on DSR are Split Multipath Routing (SMR) (Lee S-J, Gerla.M, 2001) which establishes maximum disjoint paths and Multipath Source Routing (MSR) (Wang L, Zhang L, Shu Y. Dong,2000) distributes load between multiple routes. Wei et al. proposed Robust Multipath Source Routing Protocol (RMPSR) (Wei Wei, Zakhor A, 2004) that uses a per-packet allocation scheme to distribute video packets over two primary routes of two route sets, to support Multiple Description Coding (MDC) application in MANETs. Hui-Yao et al. proposed Cluster-based multipath dynamic source routing in MANET (CMDSR) (H-Y, Zhong L, Lu X-C, Peng W., 2005) is based on 2-level hierarchical scheme that transfer the Route Discovery procedure to the 2-server level to prevent network flooding due to the DSR Route Discovery. It uses Multi-level cluster structure to improve scalability. Disjoint multipath source routing (DMPSR) (Wisitpongphan and Tonguz, 2003) allows source packets to be statistically multiplexed onto multiple disjoint routes (Wisitpongphan N, Tonguz K, 2003). Multipath energy aware on demand source routing (MEA-DSR) exploits information about energy levels of batteries for balancing energy consumption between mobile nodes.

Many recent research works focus on ensuring route discovery in Dynamic Source Routing (DSR) secure. Poonam et al. (2010) proposed a "Trust based multi path DSR protocol" which uses multi-path forwarding approach. This method forward RREQ to its neighbour only if it is received from different path. It detects and avoids misbehaving nodes which increases vulnerability in DSR route discovery. Trust based DSR routing protocol overcomes three issues such as message confidentiality, message integrity and access control(Prayag Narula a, Sanjay Kumar Dhurandher ,Sudip Misra b, Isaac Woungang, 2008). Resilient security framework scheme along with DSR routing protocol (Binod Vaidya, Dimitrios Makrakis, Jong Hyuk Park, Sang-Soo Yeo, 2011) protects message modification, fabrication, man-in-middle attack, black hole attack, invisible-node attack. Appending Statistical Analysis of Multipath (SAM) with multipath DSR protects wormhole attack, Ning Song and Lijun Qian Xiangfang Li, 2005) introduces low overhead and works with dynamic network topology.

To protect against several type of routing attack and wormhole attack watchdog technique is used (Bayrem Triki, Slim Rekhis, and Noureddine Boudriga, 2012) which detects whether neighbour nodes forward datagram as expected. False routing is protected using digital signature scheme which authenticates nodes and guarantee integrity of information.

Watchdog with DSR improves the capability of the node, by allowing it to detect attacks using local information. Broadcasting traffic increases as source node sends RREQ to all nodes in the network which in turn rises routing overhead. In this research a Dynamic MPR algorithm along with threshold based multipath routing which reduces routing overhead by placing constraint on Route discovery in DSR has been proposed.

4.5.1. Flooding Schemes

To solve the broadcast storm problem, many methods have been proposed (J. Wu and F. Dai,2004) In general, these broadcast protocols are categorized into three classes: probability-based methods, area-based methods and neighbour knowledge method. Among this the neighbour knowledge method is further classified as neighbour-designated methods and self-pruning methods. MPR (multipoint relay) comes under neighbour-designated method that exhibits both efficiency and simplicity.

There are three groups of MPR scheme namely Pure MRP, MPR-based CDS, QOS-based MPR. Pure MPR is based on the notion of original MPR selection heuristics. Several extensions are followed so as to improve some specified performances such as collision avoidance, reducing the number of generated forwarding nodes and power usage efficiency. MPR-CDS generates Connected Dominating Set that reduces number of forwarding nodes. QOS-MPR examines the QoS requirements in the network and selects the MPR which meet quality requirement of the network (Ou Liang, Y.Ahmet Sekercioglu, and Nallasamy Mani,2006). The preliminary step that aids in better supporting QoS in Ad hoc networks is to find an MPR set that could guarantee the QoS metrics such as bandwidth and delay.

4.6. Proposed Dynamic Multipath Routing Scheme

4.6.1. HELLO Message

In Multipath DSR, generally HELLO message aids in discovering neighbours. It is send periodically by a node to determine its one-hop neighbours. They are generated and transmitted to all one-hop neighbours to achieve link-sensing, neighbour-sensing, two-hop neighbour-sensing and MPR selector sensing. Two-hop HELLO message allows each node to maintain two up-to date lists, first list contains one-hop neighbours and second list contain 2-hop neighbours as detailed in (Bayrem Triki, Slim Rekhis, and Noureddine Boudriga, 2012). Nodes in the network maintain list of all nodes that are reachable via symmetric neighbours in the routing table. It helps in MPR calculation. The nodes that have been selected as MPR are informed through HELLO message.

4.6.2. *MPR Computation*

<table>
<tr><td>

Algorithm: MPR computation

Input Require: List of 1-hop neighbours N1(x), 2-hop neighbours N2(x), and their willingness

Step 1: Initially MPR(x) = 0

        add all n∈N1(x) with willingness==WILL ALWAYS to MPR(x)

        add all n∈N1(x) to MPR(x) if they are the only way to reach n ∈ N2(x)

Step 2: while not all n ∈ N2(x) can be reached via the MPR nodes do

        for each n ∈ N1(x) do

        num = number of nodes in N2(x) that are reachable via n and are not yet covered

        end for

        add n ∈ N1(x) with highest willingness or high num value to MPR(x)

        end while

Step 3: To optimize, process each n∈N1(u) in MPR(x), one at a time, andif MPR(x)-

        {n ∈ N1(x)} still covers all nodes in N2(x) then

        remove n from MPR(x).

</td></tr>
</table>

MPR flooding scheme has been incorporated in SeMuRAMAS before broadcasting RREQ by a node. 1-hop neighbour (N1(x)) and 2-hop neighbours (N2(x)) obtained through Two-hop HELLO message aids in selecting MPR nodes from list of available n nodes. If a node wants to act as an MPR node it may specify via a willingness value from 0 (WILL NEVER) to 7 (WILL ALWAYS) that has been explained by(A. Qayyum, L. Viennot, and A. Laouiti, 2002)

4.7. The Proposed Dynamic MPR(DMPR)

Dynamic Multi-Path Routing (DMPR) is an extension of MPR (Multi Point Relay). MPR has security but it is a limited broadcasting scheme where in the broadcasting traffic increases as source node sends route request (RREQ) to all nodes in the network which in turn rises routing overhead. The proposed Dynamic MPR algorithm incorporates threshold based multipath routing which reduces routing overhead by placing constraint on Route discovery in DSR. Fig 4.7 shows the proposed dynamic MPR scheme.

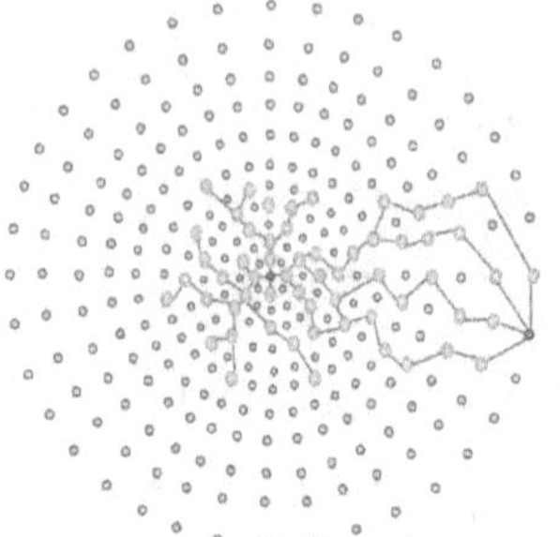

Figure 4.7: Proposed Dynamic MPR Scheme

MPR nodes within the network is found using MPR computation algorithm. Each MPR node holds a list of 1-hop and 2-hop neighbours. It executes DMPR algorithm before it starts broadcasting.

Generally, when a node receives RREQ its hop count (Hc) value is increased. Based on nhc value, the proposed algorithm places constrain in flooding process. On receiving RREQ message, each MPR node checks whether its Hc value is less than or equal to 6(Universal Hopcount), if so unconditional broadcast takes place to its neighbours. Once hop count value exceeds 6 then route cache of each MPR(x) is searched for destination (Ds), and on finding that Destination is in that route only broadcasting is made by this MPR(x) to its neighbours. In case if there is no Ds in any of the MPR(x) then nhc value is incremented and DMPR algorithm is called recursively till destination is reached.

```
Algorithm for Dynamic MPR
DMPR(MPR(x))
{
static int nhc=6;
for (each MPR(x))
 if(hc<=nhc)
      Broadcast to its neighbors;
 else
 {
   MPR_GC=0;
     for (each MPR(x))
         if( Ds is in x route cache)
             Broadcast to its neighbors;
             MPR_GC=1;
     end for
     if (MPR_GC==0)
         nhc++;
         DMPR( );}}
```

In MPR scheme, certain nodes are selected for broadcasting where as it takes place in all the direction. The proposed algorithm not only selects few nodes but also restricts the direction of broadcasting. If Ds are found on a node, DMPR start broadcasting only in that direction. Reduction in number of RREQ in turn imposes reduction in routing load. Once the broadcasting is completed source node contains multiple route that has been obtained based on threshold value for reaching destination. Source node chooses the shortest path and start forwarding the packets.

4.8. Simulation

4.8.1. Simulation Environment

The proposed approach was evaluated in an NS-2 simulation environment. To simulate a user's request behavior, assume that each mobile host generates a series of data item requests with exponentially distributed time intervals. Multipath DSR routing protocol is used for propagation in the simulation. In this section, simulation results for both DMPR and SeMuRAMAS protocols have been presented. The simulation environment consists of mobile nodes in a rectangular region.

The nodes are randomly placed in the region and each of them has a radio propagation range of meters. The channel bandwidth is assumed to be Mb/sec. Constant bit rate (CBR) flows are deployed for data transmission. All nodes have the same transmission range of 250 meters. The mobility model is the random waypoint model. The random waypoint model is commonly used for simulating the movement pattern of mobile host in a MANET. For 50 nodes the simulation was carried out in a grid of 900m x 900m similarly for 100 and 150 nodes it is carried out in a grid of 1500m x 1000m. Primary parameters used for simulation are shown in Table 1.

Table 4.1: Simulation Parameters

Parameter	Value
Transmission range(M)	250
Bandwidth(Mbps)	512
Max. Node Speed (m/s)	7
Pause Time(s)	0
Packet Size(KB)	1000
Average TTL(S)	40
Number of Data items	1000
Traffic	CBR
Simulation Time (S)	20
Number of nodes	50, 100, 150

4.8.2. *Performance Metrics*

Comparison between existing and proposed scheme is estimated based on the following metrics

Generated Packets: Total number of data packets that has been generated by source node.

Received Packets: Total number of data packets that has been received by destination node.

Packet Delivery Ratio (PDR): It is defined as the ratio of number of packets received to that of number of packets send. If this rate is high then reliability of network is high.

Routing Load: It is defined as the ratio of number of routing packets send to that of number of data packets received. If routing load is high then throughput of the network is low.

CBR Bytes: Total size of data packets in bytes received at the destination. Route bytes: Total size of control packets in bytes transmitted by source and intermediate node. Route cost: It is defined as the ratio of Route bytes to that of CBR byte.

The values that are obtained from the experiment are listed in Table 2. Performance of the existing SeMuRAMAS scheme and the proposed DMPR scheme under different network size such as 50, 100 and 150 nodes has been analyzed. From the results it is seen that the proposed scheme generates low routing load than the existing scheme under all scenario. DMPR broadcast only in the direction of destination. Hence the routing load caused by the proposed scheme in 50 nodes is less compared to that in SeMuRAMAS. This in turn reduces the number of control packet used for finding multiple routes.

Table 4.2: Simulated Data

Simulation Setup	DMPR			SeMuRAMAS		
No. of nodes	50	100	150	50	100	150
PDR	96.06	85.71	95	90.9	71.83	89.01
Dropped Packets	7	12	10	12	20	10
Routing Load	0.16	0.93	0.91	0.53	2.86	2.01
CBR Bytes	171000	72000	115000	120000	51000	81000
Route bytes	2536	8384	8200	5252	12828	14816
Route Costs	0.01	0.19	0.17	0.04	0.25'	0.18

According to DMPR scheme, initially RREQ packet size is 32 byte. Packet header of RREQ keeps on increasing as the length of the route extends. During route discovery, DMPR floods RREQ with initial packet size. The results show that the proposed scheme have flooded only 2536 route bytes, that is used to find the path on which 171000 data packets were transmitted, where as SeMuRAMAS floods 5252 route bytes to transmit 120000 data packets. DMPR has flooded less route bytes than SeMuRAMAS so, bandwidth consumption is also low. It is also seen that in all three scenarios, the existing scheme makes use of large amount of route bytes to transmit fewer amount of data packets that cause increase in route cost and routing load. In the proposed scheme, the number of packets that has been dropped is less when compared to that of existing scheme. This in turn increases packet delivery ratio of DMPR.

4.8.3. *Experimental Result*

Packet Delivery Ratio (PDR)

The following chart illustrates the performance evaluation between SeMuRAMAS and DMPR algorithms with respect to packet delivery ratio for 50, 100 and 150 nodes.

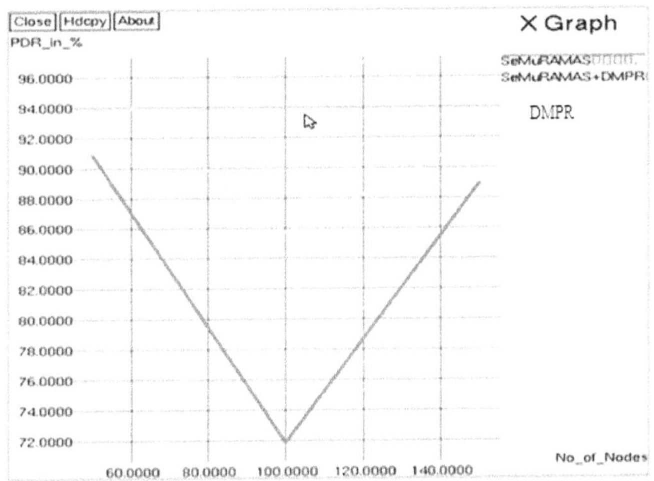

Figure 4.8: PDR between SeMuRAMAS and DMPR

It is observed from Figure 4.8 that Packet Delivery Ratio (PDR) of 50 nodes using SeMuRAMAS is 90.9% and using DMPR is 96.6%, PDR of 100 nodes using SeMuRAMAS is 71.83% and using DMPR is 85.71% . For 150, nodes PDR using SeMuRAMAS is 89.01% and DMPR is 95%.

It is observed from the results that value of PDR drops in 100 nodes but regains in 150 nodes which means that PDR significantly changes when the number of nodes varies. From the experimental results it is also observed that the proposed DMPR algorithm is maintaining higher PDR compared to SeMuRAMAS, which shows the efficiency of the proposed method.

Route Overhead

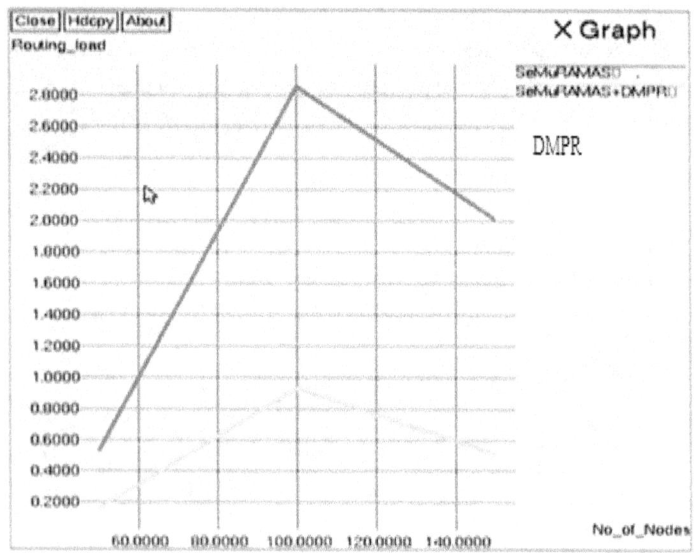

Figure 4.9: Routing Overhead between SeMuRAMAS and DMPR

Figure 4.9 illustrates the routing overhead performance evaluation of SeMuRAMAS and DMPR algorithms on 50, 100 and 150 nodes. From the results it is proved that the routing overhead of 50 nodes using SeMuRAMASis 0.53 and using DMPR is 0.16. Routing overhead node of 100 nodes using SeMuRAMAS is 2.86 and using DMPR is 0.93. For 150 nodes, the routing overhead using SeMuRAMAS is 2.01 and using DMPR is 0.91. It is observed from the results that the routing overhead is considerably less in DMPR algorithm in all scenarios. From the experimental results it is also observed that the proposed DMPR algorithm out performs SeMuRAMASon route overhead.

Route Cost

Figure 4.10 illustrates the comparison of routing cost between SeMuRAMAS and DMPR.

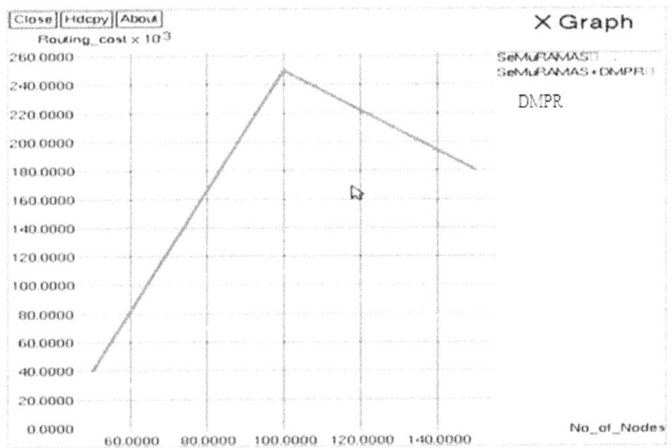

Figure 4.10: Routing Cost between SeMuRAMAS and DMPR

The results show that the route cost of SeMuRAMAS are0.04 at 50 nodes, 0.25 at 100 nodes and 0.18 at 150 nodes, whereas the route cost using DMPR are 0.01 at 50 nodes, 0.19 at 100 nodes and 0.17 at 150 nodes. It is observed from the results that the route cost is comparatively low in DMPR algorithm in all scenarios.

Bandwidth consumption is based on size of the data to be transmitted. Each control packet has its own packet size. In case large amount of data is to be transmitted using more control packets will cause additional overhead. To rectify this, either the size of control packet is to be reduced or there should be limitation in use of routing packets. In the proposed method this is achieved by reduction of routing packets which limits broadcasting. The experimental results illustrate that DMPR is more efficient than SeMuRAMAS in terms of packet delivery ratio, routing load and route cost.

4.9.   Summary

MANET has various constraints before transmitting successful data. In the proposed DMPR, special features have been incorporated on route discovery. The experimental results have proved that the proposed DMPR algorithm performs better on routing overhead, routing cost and packet delivery ratio. Thereby secured broadcast mechanism with reduced routing overhead on DSR protocol is ensured.

CHAPTER 5

QUADRANT BASED ROUTING SCHEME

Quadrant based secured multipath routing scheme (QRS)in MASNET environment has been developed to reduce the broadcasting time.

5.1. Introduction

Mobile Ad-hoc Networks (MANETs) are generally defined as infrastructure-less environment with frequent change in network topology. But, recently many of its routing protocols have used the Global Positioning System (GPS) to quicken the node discovery process. GPS delivers the position of mobile nodes, which can be further used to compute the routing path. Therefore, the routing protocols can reduce greater part of overheads effectively. Similarly, equipping Wireless Sensor Nodes (WSN) with GPS receivers are widely available solutions.

To use GPS, a node must be equipped with a GPS receiver which is responsible for estimating the absolute position of the node in the global coordinate system. Though GPS makes it possible to provide a wide range of positioning services, it is not a completely viable solution for ad hoc networks due to its additional hardware support, cost, and power consumption. A wide variety of routing protocols aim to localize the ad hoc network without the support of GPS have been proposed over the years. LAR protocol is a location aided routing protocol which uses location information to reduce the search space for a desired route and limiting the search space results in fewer route discovery messages.

5.2. Location Aided Routing (LAR) Protocol

LAR is an on-demand routing protocol whose function is analogous to Dynamic Source Routing (DSR) (Soliman, H. and M. AlOtaibi, 2009).Quite the opposite of DSR, LAR protocol makes use of geological location information to restrict the area for finding a new route to a smaller request zone. In its place of flooding the route requests interested in the whole network, only those nodes in the request zone will forward them.

5.2.1. Route Discovery Using Flooding

The LAR routing protocol uses flooding technique to send the route request message to all its neighbors. The following figure 5.1 illustrates the flooding technique used in LAR protocol (Y. B. Ko and N. H. Vaidya,2000).

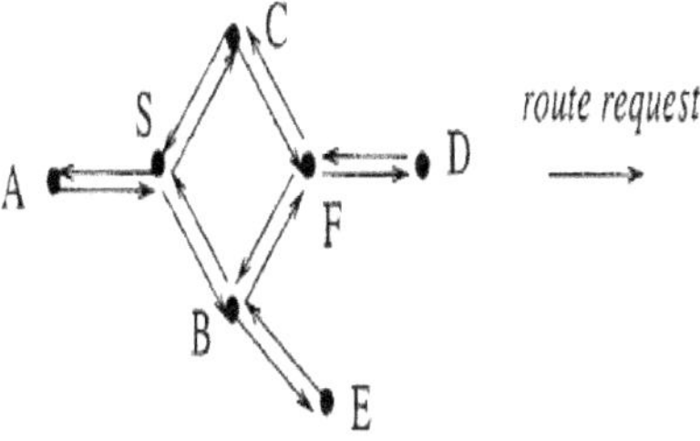

Figure 5.1: Flooding Sequence in LAR

In the above figure, node S needs to determine a route to node D. Therefore, node S broadcasts a route request to its neighbours. When node B and C receive the route request, they forward it to all their neighbours. When node F receives the route request from B, it forwards the request to its neighbours. However, when node F receives the same route request from C, node F simply discards the route request.

As the route request is propagated to various nodes, the path followed by the request is included in the route request packet. Using the above flooding algorithm, provided that the intended destination is reachable from the sender, the destination should eventually receive a route request message.

On receiving the route request, the destination responds by sending a route reply message to the sender –the route reply message follows a path that is obtained by reversing the path followed by the route request received by D (the route request message includes the path traversed by the request).

It is possible that the destination will not receive a route request message (for instance, when it is unreachable from the sender or route requests are lost due to transmission errors). In such cases, the sender needs to be able to reinitiate route discovery. Therefore, when a sender initiates route discovery, it sets a timeout. If during the timeout interval, a route reply is not received, then a new route discovery is initiated (the route request messages for this route discovery will use a different sequence number than the previous route discovery – recall that sequence numbers are useful to detect multiple receptions of the same route request). Timeout may occur if the destination does not receive a route request, or if the route reply message from the destination is lost.

Route discovery is initiated either when the sender S detects that a previously determined route to node D is broken, or if S does not know a route to the destination. In our implementation, we assume that node S can know that the route is broken only if it attempts to use the route. When node S sends a data packet along a particular route, a node along that path returns a route error message, if the next hop on the route is broken. When node S receives the route error message, it initiates route discovery for destination D. When using this technique, the route request would reach every node that is reachable from node S (potentially, all nodes in the ad hoc network). Using location information, we attempt to reduce the number of nodes to whom route request is propagated.

The Location-Aided Routing (LAR), makes use of location information to reduce routing overhead. Location information used in the LAR protocol may be provided by the Global Positioning System (GPS) (B.W. Parkinson and S.W. Gilbert, NAVSTAR,1983). With the availability of GPS, it is possible for a mobile host to know its physical location.

In reality, position information provided by GPS includes some amount of error, which is the difference between GPS-calculated coordinates and the real coordinates. For instance, NAVSTAR Global Positioning System has positional accuracy of about 50–100 m and Differential GPS offers accuracies of a few meters.

5.2.2. LAR Routing Function

To find out the request zone, there are two schemes. In the initial one, the source calculates a circular area (expected zone) in which the destination is predictable to be found at the current time. The position and the size of the circle are estimated based on the location information of the preceding destination, the time on the spot associated with the previous location record and the average speed of the destination as seen in Figure 5.2. The request zone is a small rectangular region that comprises of the expected zone and the source. The coordinates of the four corners are incorporated in the route request packet at what time commencing the route discovery process. RREQ broadcast is limited to this request zone. Therefore, when a node in the request zone receives RREQ, it forwards the packet in general. But when a node which is not in the request zone receives an RREQ, it drops the packet. For instance, in (Figure 5.2), if node I receives the route request from some another node, the node I forwards the request to its neighbors node, because I, decide that it is surrounded by the rectangular request zone. Despite the fact that, when node J receives the route request, it rejects the request, as node J is not inside the request zone.

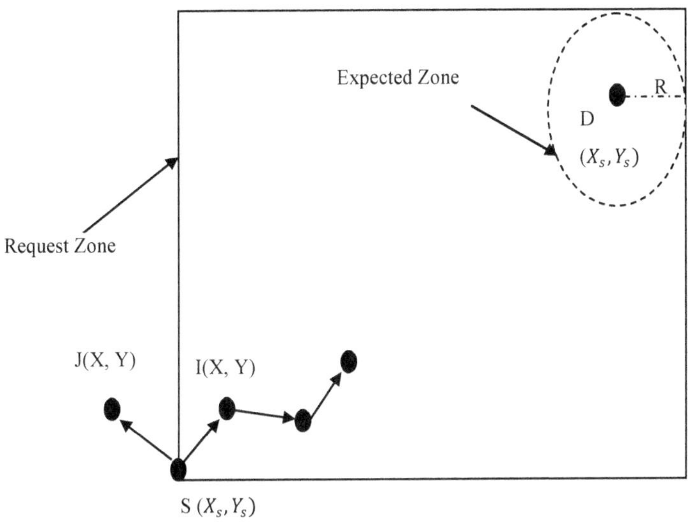

Figure 5.2: Standard LAR Scheme 1

If source node S knows a previous location of destination node D at time t_0, if it also knows its average speed v and the current time t_l, then the expected zone at time t_l is a circle around P with radius $R = v^*(t_l - t_0)$. Once the destination D receives the route request packet, it sends back a route reply packet as in the flooding algorithms. Its reply differs by containing its current position, the actual time, and its average speed. Source node S is available to make use of this information for a route discovery in the future. In the second scheme, the source calculates the distance to the destination based on the location of the destination. This distance, is integrated in the route request message and sent to neighbors. When an intermediate node receives the request, it calculates its distance to the destination. It will relay the request only if its distance to the destination is less than the distance included in the request message.

The LAR scheme effectively reduces the broadcasting region. In order to further reduce the broadcasting sequence, a new quadrant based protocol has been proposed in this research work.

5.3.   Quadrant

In mathematics, a sector one quarter of a circle or sector of a two dimensional Cartesian coordinate system is referred as quadrant. The following figure illustrates the quadrant.

The WSN and MANETs often use the base station temporary infrastructure to carry out the entire operation. In such a case, total network coverage area can be computed using collection of neighbouring coordinates. Therefore, among the network coverage area, the source node S and destination node D can be anywhere around the network coverage area. The proposed Qudarant Routing Scheme internally uses LAR protocol to receive the location information of a node or collection of nodes.

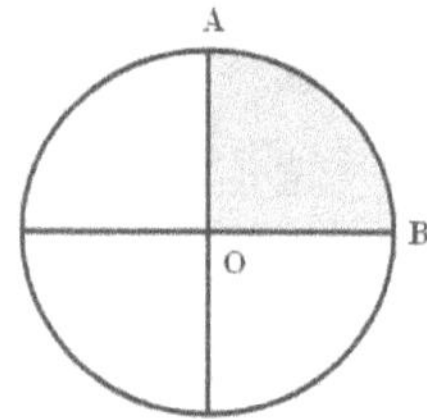

Figure 5.3: Quadrant Example

According to the specification, various scenarios can be derived, such as source node S and destination node D can be in the same quadrant, node S and node D can be in adjacent quadrants or node S and node D can be in the reciprocal quadrant. The QRS algorithm will finds the physical locations and restricts the original network range to the selected quadrants. The following section describes the QRS algorithm.

5.4.   QRS Algorithm

The proposed routing algorithm enforces the route discovery process in conjunction with LAR and Secured Multipath Routing. Six kinds of datagram are used by QRS during the route discovery.

- Route Request datagram: It is the first packet to be broadcasted by a mobile node which wants to establish a multipath route to the destination mobile node. Every intermediate node exploits this datagram to discover incomplete routes in the network. It also appends it's identity in the RREQ and broadcasts it to its neighbours.

- Route Response datagram: If the information is sent back by the destination mobile node upon reception of the RREQ. This datagram contains the optimal path and is source routed to the node which generated the RREQ.

- Notification datagram: It is used by the destination node to ask the intermediate nodes to forward the information they have learned regarding the routes to the source node. The information is invisible to the destination mobile node when it receives the RREQ datagram.

- List forwarding datagram: It is used by the intermediate nodes to forward the information that is stored regarding the existing paths in the network.

- Route Error datagram: It is sent by an intermediate node to the source node when it detects a route failure. It also lets the source node update the set of paths it uses to reach the destination mobile node.

- Threshold tuning datagram: It is used by an intermediate node to indicate the value by which the threshold should be increased to let the establishment of the requested multiple paths to be possible.

Network Discovery: When a mobile node, say S1, joins the network, it broadcasts a two-hop HELLO message, which includes its identity and has a Time To Live (TTL) value equal to 2 along with location information (*Xi , Yi*) and timestamp *t*. Any node, say S2, which hears the message, includes the identity of S1 in its list of one-hop neighbours, sets the TTL value of the HELLO message equal to 1 lower than its received value, and forwards the datagram. Any node, say S3 that hears the message includes the identity of S2 in its list of one-hop neighbours and S1 in its list of two-hop neighbours, sets the TTL value of the HELLO message equal to 1 lower than its received value, and discards the datagram. To be considered as active, every node should periodically send a two-hop HELLO message and follow the above described process. This allows each node to maintain two up-to-date lists. The first is the list of neighbours and the second shows for each neighbour the list of its neighbours. The two lists will support the detection of routing attacks.

Route Request Generation and Forwarding: A node which wants to establish a path to the destination mobile node say DN, initiates the route discovery by generating a RREQ datagram to DN, and broadcasting it in the network. Prior to initiating the route discovery process, the following steps are involved: first step extracts the network space where the SN and DN belongs. In this case, we assume the network space as circular pattern, hence using circular sector formula the network space is divided into four regions.

$$A = \pi r^2 \cdot \frac{\theta^\circ}{360}$$

The region labels are nominated for each region in anticlockwise direction as Q1, Q2, Q3 and Q4. Now it initiates the second step, which tries to identify the regions where the SN, DN nodes belong. In this case minimum one region and maximum Qn – 1 regions may be selected for limiting the total network space. Hence at this point, the proposed broadcasting scheme will save atleast of 25% network space and eliminates the nodes belonging to the region. The third step triggers to limit the network region and the fourth step broadcast the RREQ to all nodes belonging to the selected regions. Figure 5.4 illustrates the region.

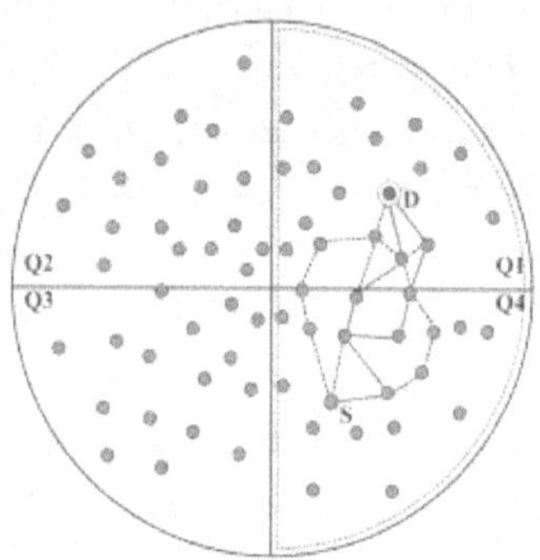

Figure 5.4: QRS Broadcasting Scheme

Every generated RREQ includes five-tuple information: <Seq, RREC, Dt, Loc, Region>. Seq stands for a sequence number which should be different for every new generated RREQ. The sequence number together with the IP address of the sender allows to uniquely identifying the RREQ and associates it to the subsequent generated responses. Dt is the disjointness threshold which is set by the sender to specify the maximal number of nodes that could be shared by any two paths among the set of paths to establish with the destination node. The value of Dt remains unchanged during the forwarding of the RREQ to the destination. RREC is a route record which is used to include the path followed by the RREQ to reach *DN*. In fact, when a node in the network receives a copy of this datagram for the first time, it appends its identity to the RREC field, broadcasts it to its neighbors. Every node, say *N*, including *DN*, which receives a second copy of the datagram, extracts the content of the RREC field. The latter provides a path from the sender to the node *N*. The node *N* will append the content of RREC together with the value of *Seq* to a list stored locally, entitled *RP*, which stands for list of Received Paths. Then it discards the datagram. Loc contains the location information *Xi,Yi,ti* and Region refers the limited region to be broadcasted the RREQ.

Route Response Generation and Forwarding: Once different copies of the RREQ datagram reach the destination node, the latter will generate a Route Response datagram, say RREP, to the source. It includes four-tuple information <Seq, R, RCN, RPBS> where Seq represents the value of the sequence number that appeared within the received RREQ, R is the route, which is composed of the sequence of nodes identities representing the shortest path (between the source and the destination mobile node DN) among those that were received within the different copies of the RREQs. RCN stands for the remaining number of common nodes. It is initiated by DN to the value of X received within the RREQ. This value is decreased by 1 every time the RREP is routed by a node which contains a non empty list of received paths for the same value of the sequence number. The RREP datagram will be source routed to the sender based on the content of R. Moreover a list, say RPBS, containing the list of all the routing paths connecting the source node to DN is added to the RREP. When the RREP packet is routed to the source, the latter and all intermediate nodes will discover a route to DN, store it in their cache, and use it as an alternative path if some link error will potentially occur. We remind the reader that any different routes requests, to be received by DN may share some nodes. Every route can be written as a series of nodes shared with other routes, followed by a series of distinct nodes.

Notification Datagrams Generation and Forwarding: In the case where the destination mobile node MD has discarded a copy of the RREQ, it generates a notification datagram, say ND, containing the four-tuple information <Seq, RCN, L, RPBS> composed of the sequence number (Seq) and the value of RCN received in the RREP, in addition to a list L containing the identities of neighbour nodes from which a received copy of the RREQ was previously discarded (i.e., the identities of these neighbours stand for the last nodes in the routing paths provided by RP and related to the sequence number Seq). In the case where the ND is sent by the BS, the list L will be set to the identities of neighbour nodes from which a copy of the RREQ was received. RPBS is a list containing the set of routing paths connecting the source node to DN, including the shortest path. These routes are collected from the copies of the RREQ received by DN. The notification datagram ND is sent to the source node, broadcasted but treated only by nodes existing in the list L.

In the case where some node X in the network receives the RREP, two situations may happen. If X has already discarded at least one copy of the related RREQ, it forwards it after decreasing the value of RCN and generates an ND containing the four-tuple information <Seq, RCN – 1, L, RPBS>. If it is not the case, it simply forwards the datagram to its neighbours. When the intermediate node X receives a Notification datagram ND for the first time, two situations may happen. If X has not previously discarded any copy of the related RREQ, it simply forwards the NP to its neighbours.

If X has already discarded at least one copy of the related RREQ, it forwards it after decreasing the value of RNC and replacing the value of L by the identities of neighbour nodes from which a received copy of the RREQ was previously discarded. When X receives a second copy of the ND, it simply discards it. If the value RNC becomes equal to 0 after decreasing it by one, the notification packet will be rejected before sending it.

List Forwarding Datagrams Generation and Forwarding: Every node, which decreases the RCN's value of the Notification Datagram ND, generates a list forwarding datagram containing the sequence number (already received in the ND) and a list obtained from RP (the sequence number associated to RP should be the same as the one received in the ND) after applying two filters, say F1 and F2, consecutively. The list forwarding datagram is sent to the source node (i.e., the node which initiated the RREQ). The first filter F1 eliminates from RP any path that has more than RCN–1 shared nodes with any path existing in RPBS. The second filter F2 locates in the output of F1 groups of nodes that share more than RCN –1 nodes. It replaces each one of these groups in the RP list by the shortest path. When the source node specifies a disjointness threshold x equal to 0 (i.e., all the discovered paths must be disjoint), the ND will be sent with a value of RCN equal to 0. Intermediate nodes receiving this latter and having an empty RP, should forward the packet to their neighbours. If it is not the case, they drop the notification datagram ND. Each time a node sends its RP list to the source node, it eliminates this list from its memory to preserve storage resources. If there is no additional space in the node memory, a solution consists in using the neighbour memory. Two categories of nodes can be used: nodes with high storage capacity and nodes with limited storage capacity. Each node knows the category of its neighbours. A node with a low storage capacity has the possibility to send parts of the data it stores only to neighbour nodes with high storage capacity. In fact, the receiving node should send back the data to the sender before it goes out of its coverage or sleeps. If the sender memory is still full, the receiving node should find a neighbour node, which is also a neighbour of the sender and has a high storage capacity, transfer the data to that node, and inform the sender about its identity.

Threshold Tuning Datagram Generation and Forwarding: Each time a mobile node sets the RCN to 0, it executes filters F1 and F2 of the content of the RP to discard paths exceeding, in terms of shared nodes, the authorized disjointness threshold. The mobile node computes the minimal number of shared nodes says n, between the remaining paths in the RP and sends this value to the source node within the TTD datagram. This value could be exploited by the source node, in the case where it is unable to establish the set of paths satisfying the requested threshold. It determines the best suitable threshold value that could be guaranteed by the network topology. This value will equal be n greater than the last used threshold value. The subsequent section discuss about the limiting network space using QRS scheme.

5.4.1. QRS Limiting Network Space

```
// Limiting Network Space through QUAD broadcasting scheme
QUAD_LNS (Network Space, SN, DN)
{
    Find center point of the network space and radius;
    Classify the network space into quad format Q1,Q2,Q3,Q4;
    Evaluate the region of source and destination nodes;
    If (SN_Region == DN_Region)
    {
        // Limiting the network region
        Lm_Region = SN_Region;
        Return the Lm_Region;
    }
    // if SN_Region is adjacent to DN_Region either way
    Else if (SN_edge == DN_edge)
    {
        // Merging of selected regions
        Lm_Region = SN_Region + DN Region;
        Return the Lm_Region;
    }
    Else
        {
        Predict the distance of DN from two adjacent
        quads of SN;
        // Intermediate Region
        Im_Region = Region has Less distance to DN;
        // Merging of selected regions
        Lm_Region = SN_Region + DN_Region + Im_Region;
        Return the Lm_Region;
        }
}
```

The algorithm establishes that network range can be observed from the density of nodes in the network. Therefore, it is required to find out the center point and radius of the network space. The next step involves in slicing the network space based on the available information into quadruple format and assigns the region label. The algorithm then triggers to evaluate the region where SN and DN nodes belong. If both SN_region and DN_region are same, it returns the Lm_region as SN_region; thus the original broadcasting range is limited to the specific range.

Otherwise, SN_region and DN_region are compared as adjacent region in either way. If both are adjacent, now the Lm_region tries to merge the SN_region & DN_region and return the Lm_region as limited network space. If the preceding conditions fail, it means that SN_region and DN_region belong to opposite direction. Hence, this sequence is not advised to merge because center portion of the merging effect will be a narrow band. In this scenario, the chances of communication between inter-region nodes are nearly impossible. Thus, intermediate region should be formed to avoid such kind of situation. In this case, we have two intermediate regions and the selection of appropriate region is measured in terms of distance function between neighbouring region and DN. Less distance indicates the closeness to the intermediate region. Therefore SN_region, Im_region and DN_region are merged together as single limited network space. Subsequent section discuss about the simulation results and discussion. A set of security mechanisms based on the use of Watchdog and digital signature are used to protect the route discovery process.

5.5. Experimental Results

The proposed QRS multipath routing algorithm and the existing SeMuRAMAS algorithms were tested in NS-2 simulation environment. The simulation environment consists of mobile nodes in a rectangular region size meters by meters. The nodes are randomly placed in the region and each of them has a radio propagation range of meters. The channel bandwidth is assumed to be Mb/sec. The Constant Bit Rate (CBR) flows are deployed for data transmission. All nodes have the same transmission range of 250 meters. The mobility model is the random waypoint model, which is commonly used for simulating the movement pattern of mobile host in a MASNET. For 50 nodes the simulation was carried out in a grid of 900m × 900m size. The experiment is conducted using 100 nodes and 150 nodes for 1200m and 1500m range.Every node periodically floods a message throughout the entire field. Low flooding rate has been chosen to minimize the packet loss due to buffer overflows and interference. All results generated from the simulation are based on the average runs of uniform node distributions Table 5.1 depicts the basic parameters considered for this simulation.

Table 5.1: Simulation Setup

Parameters	Value
Transmission range (M)	250
Bandwidth (Mbps)	512
Max. node speed (m/s)	7
Pause time (s)	0
Packet size (KB)	1000
Average TTL (s)	40
Number of data items	1000
Traffic	CBR
Simulation time (s)	20
Number of nodes	50, 100, 150

Performance of QRS is compared with the existing SeMuRAMAS in terms of Packet Delivery Ratio (PDR) and memory overhead. PDR is the ratio of number of packets received to that of number of packets generated. If this rate is high then reliability of network is high. Similarly Routing load and route cost are also evaluated.

Table 5.2: Results for PDR in SeMuRAMAS and QRS

Parameters	Nodes		
No. of nodes	50	100	150
PDR – SeMuRAMAS	90.90	71.83	89.01
PDR – QRS	94.5	96.06	96.06

Table 5.2 shows the performance of the proposed QRS and SeMuRAMAS under 50, 100 and 150 nodes. The results show that 90.9 percent PDR is achieved at 50 nodes, but in 100 & 150 nodes the PDR is reduced to 71.83 & 89.01 in SeMuRAMAS whereas QRS achieves 94.5, 96.06 and 96.06 respectively. The QRS routing performs better compared to SeMuRAMAS. The routing load in both the methods persistently increases when the number of nodes increases. But the ratio of increase is not identical.

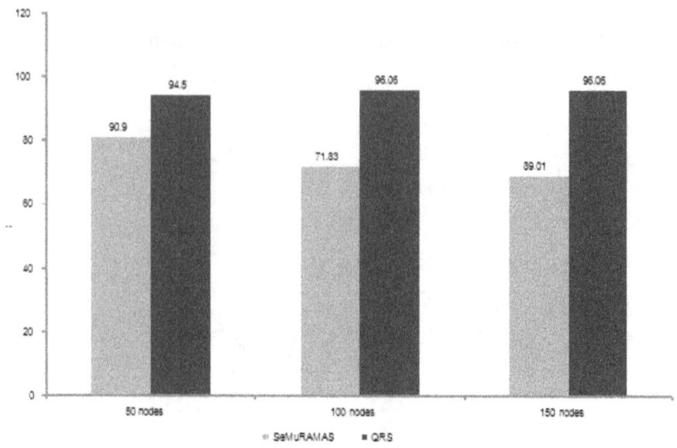

Figure 5.5: Comparison of PDR

Figure 5.5 show that QRS system has high packet delivery ratio when compared with existing SeMuRAMAS technique. From the graph, it is observed that the proposed QRS is more efficient on packet delivery ratio compared to SeMuRAMAS.

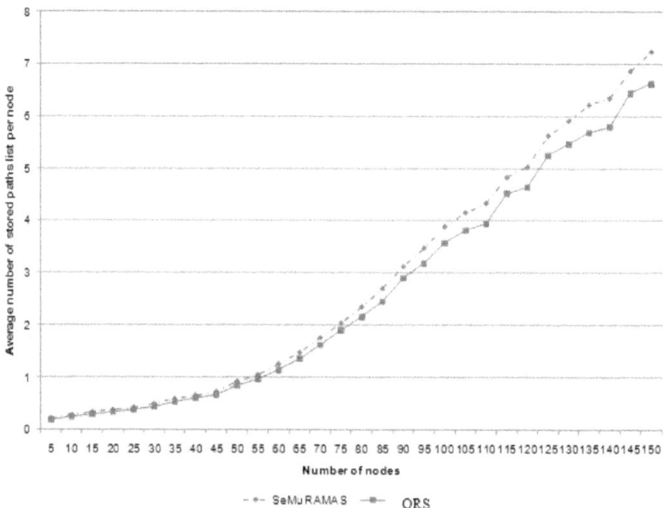

Figure 5.6: Comparison of Memory Overhead

The Figure 5.6 shows the performance of memory overhead of SeMuRAMAS & QRS. When the RREQ datagram is forwarded, every node which received a copy stores the route record in its list of received paths. Since this list is temporarily stored within the mobile node memory, the average number of stored paths in each node is estimated in terms of the number of nodes. The efficiency of 7.56% of on memory overhead handlings is achieved by QRS.

5.6.   Summary

The proposed Quadrant based multipath routing protocol is developed, which enhance the existing method SeMuRAMAS. LAR is used to embed the location information in the routing packet. Further, the QRS scheme is applied to reduce the network space by QUAD_LNS sequence between source and destination nodes. A set of security mechanisms, based on the use of Watchdog and digital signature, are used to protect the route discovery process. The performance of the proposed QRS algorithm has been analyzed. From the simulation results obtained, it is observed that the QRS algorithm performs better in terms of route discovery phase than SeMuRAMAS. QRS scheme also reduces the routing overhead as well as maintains security in multipath environment.

CHAPTER 6

RECTANGLE ZONE BASED LOCATION SPECIFIC ROUTING SCHEME

Rectangular Zone Based Location Specific Routing Scheme (RZLSR) is a multipath routing scheme proposed for MASNET environment. RZLSR algorithm is an extension of LAR protocol with tilted rectangle region for limiting the broadcasting area. The proposed algorithm improves the efficiency of routing overhead, throughput and packet delivery ratio.

6.1. Introduction

In general, MANET and WSN are sharing the similar idea on routing scheme. The proposed RZLSR algorithm is an extension of location aided routing (LAR) protocol with tilted rectangular region for limiting the existing broadcasting area.

6.2. Rectangle Zone

The LAR protocol is one of the efficient methods in handling the route discovery processes. With an association of Global Positioning System (GPS), it is possible to extract the physical location of the mobile node. In reality, the data sent by the GPS and physical position of the mobile node may find some error. But, we have considered the data sent by GPS as core for assessment.

The LAR algorithm (Y. B. Ko and N. H. Vaidy) uses two zones known as request zone and expected zone.

Expected Zone: Consider a node S that needs to find a route to node D. Assume that node S knows that node D was at location L at time t_0, and that the current time is t_1. Then, the "expected zone" of node D, from the viewpoint of node S at time t_1, is the region that node S expects to contain node D at time t_1. Node S can determine the expected zone based on the knowledge that node D was at location L at time t_0. For instance, if node S knows that node D travels with average speed v, then S may assume that the expected zone is the circular region of radius v $(t_1 - t_0)$, centered at location L (see figure 6.1(a)). If actual speed happens to be larger than the average, then the destination may actually be outside the expected zone at time t_1. Thus, expected zone is only an estimate made by node S to determine a region that potentially contains D at time t_1. In general, it is also possible to define v to be the maximum speed (instead of the average) or some other measure of the speed distribution.

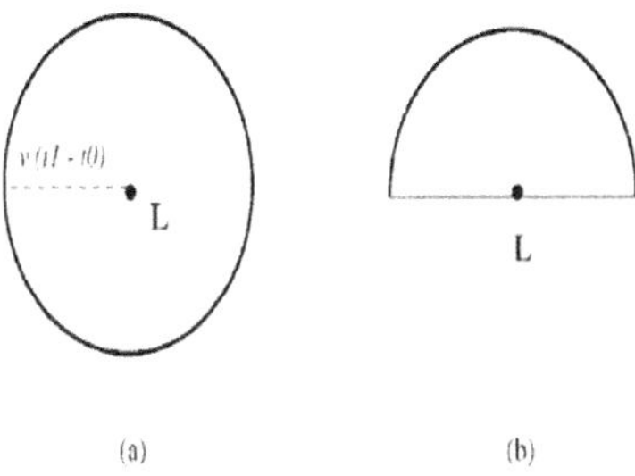

Figure 6.1: Expected Zone Example

If node S does not know a previous location of node D, then node S cannot reasonably determine the expected zone – in this case, the entire region that may potentially be occupied by the ad hoc network is assumed to be the expected zone. In this case, our algorithm reduces to the basic flooding algorithm. In general, having more information regarding mobility of a destination node, can result in a smaller expected zone. For instance, if S knows that destination D is moving north, then the circular expected zone in figure 6.1(a) can be reduced to a semi-circle, as in figure 6.1(b).

Request Zone: Again, consider node S that needs to determine a route to node D. The proposed LAR algorithm use flooding with one modification. Node S defines (implicitly or explicitly) a request zone for the route request.

A node forwards a route request only if it belongs to the request zone. To increase the probability that the route request will reach node D, the request zone should include the expected zone (described above). Additionally, the request zone may also include other regions around the request zone. There are two reasons for this:

- When the expected zone does not include host S, a path from host S to host D must include hosts outside the expected zone. Therefore, additional region must be included in the request zone, so that S and D both belong to the request zone (as shown in figure 6.2(a)).

- The request zone in figure 6.2(a) includes the expected zone from figure 6.1(a). In the example in figure 6.2(b), all paths from S to D include hosts that are outside the request zone. Thus, there is no guarantee that a path can be found consisting only of the hosts in a chosen request zone. Therefore, if a route is not discovered within a suitable timeout period, our protocol allows S to initiate a new route discovery with an expanded request zone–in our simulations, the expanded zone includes the entire network space. In this event, however, the latency in determining the route to D will be longer (as more than one round of route request propagation will be needed).

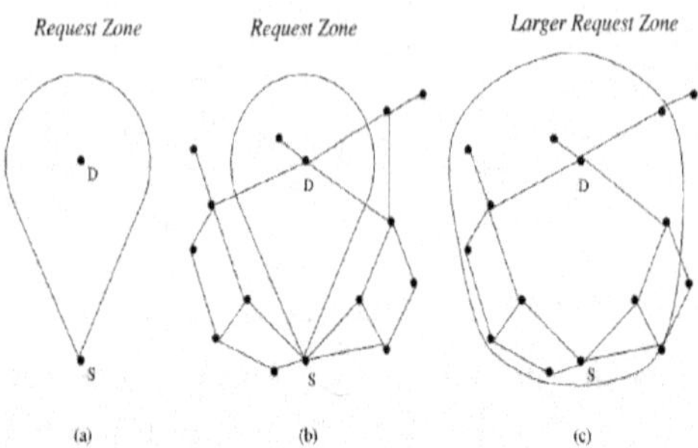

Figure 6.2: Request Zone

The probability of finding a path (in the first attempt) can be increased by increasing the size of the initial request zone (as in figure 6.2(c)). However, route discovery overhead also increases with the size of the request zone. Thus, there exists a trade-off between latency of route determination and the message overhead.

6.3.   LAR based Rectangular Zone

LAR algorithms are essentially identical to flooding, with the modification that a node that is not in the request zone does not forward a route request to its neighbours (J. Broch, D.A. Maltz, D.B. Johnson, Y.C. Hu and J. Jetcheva,1998). Thus, implementing LAR algorithm requires that a node be able to determine if it is in the request zone for a particular route request.Two LAR algorithms are presented.

The first scheme uses a request zone that is rectangular in shape (Figure 6.3 & Figure 6.4). Assume that node S knows that node D was at location (X_d, Y_d) at time t_0. At time t_1, node S initiates a new route discovery for destination D. It is also assumed that node S also knows the average speed v with which D can move. Using this, node S defines the expected zone at time t_1 to be the circle of radius $R = v (t_1 - t_0)$ centered at location (X_d, Y_d). (Instead of the average speed, v may be chosen to be the maximum speed or some other function of the speed distribution). In the LAR algorithm, the request zone will be smallest rectangle that includes current location of S and the expected zone (the circular region defined above), such that the sides of the rectangle are parallel to the X and Y axes. In figure 6.3, the request zone is the rectangle whose corners are S, A, B and C, whereas in figure 6.4, the rectangle has corners at point A, B, C and G – note that, in this figure, current location of node S is denoted as (Xs, Ys).

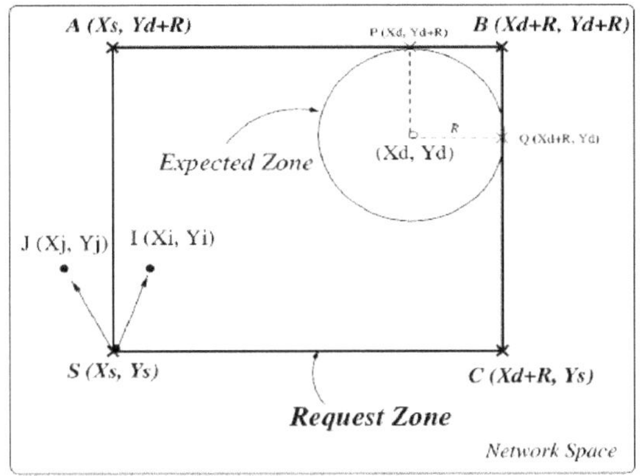

Figure 6.3: LAR Scheme 1–Source Node outside the Expected Zone

The source node S can, thus, determine the four corners of the request zone. S includes their coordinates with the route request message transmitted when initiating route discovery. When a node receives a route request, it discards the request if the node is not within the rectangle specified by the four corners included in the route request. For instance, in figure 6.3, if node I receives the route request from another node, node I forwards the request to its neighbors, because I determines that it is within the rectangular request zone. However, when node J receives the route request, node J discards the request, as node J is not within the request zone (see figure 6.3).

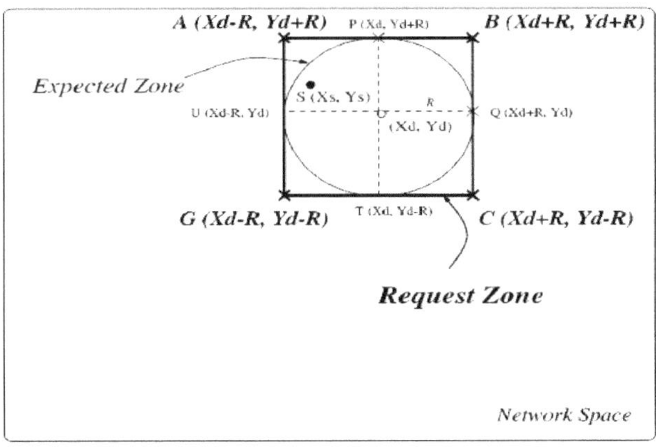

Figure 6.4: LAR Scheme II – Source Node within the Expected Zone

When node D receives the route request message, it replies by sending a route reply message (as in the flooding algorithm). However, in case of LAR, node D includes its current location and current time in the route reply message. When node S receives this route reply message (ending its route discovery), it records the location of node D. Node S can use this information to determine the request zone for a future route discovery. (It is also possible for D to include its current speed, or average speed over a recent time interval, with the route reply message. This information could be used in a future route discovery. In the proposed algorithm, it is assumed that all nodes know each other's average speed.

Size of the Request Zone: The size of the rectangular request zone above is proportional to (i) average speed of movement v, and (ii) time elapsed since the last known location of the destination was recorded. In the implementation, the sender comes to know location of the destination only at the end of a route discovery. At low speeds, route discoveries occur after long intervals, because routes break less often (thus, $t_1 - t_0$ is large). So, although factor (i) above is small, factor (ii) becomes large at low speeds, potentially resulting in a larger request zone. At high speeds as well, for similar reasons, a large request zone may be observed.

In general, a smaller request zone may occur at speeds that are neither too small, nor too large. For low speeds, it is possible to reduce the size of the request zone by piggybacking the location information on other packets, in addition to route replies.

6.4.   RZLSR Algorithm

The RZLSR algorithm is constructed using alternative definition of request zone mentioned in the LAR protocol. Sender node S may be on the border of the zone (refer figure 6.3. Instead, one may define a larger rectangle as the request zone. Also, in LAR scheme 1, the sides of the rectangle are always parallel to the X and Y axes. It is possible to remove this restriction when defining the rectangular region. For instance, one side of the rectangle may be made parallel to the line connecting the location of node S to previous location of D – this approach would often result in a smaller request zone (see figure 6.5).

Accuracy of a request zone (i.e., probability of finding a route to the destination) can be improved by adapting the request zone, initially determined by the source node S, with up-to-date location information for host D, which can be acquired at some intermediate nodes. Let us consider the case that node S starts search of a destination node D within a request zone Z at time t_1, which is based on location information about D learned by S at time t_0. Let us assume that the route request includes the timestamp t_0, because the location of node D at time t_0 is used to determine the request zone. Also, location of node S and the time t_1 when the request is originated are also included. Now suppose that some intermediate node I within Z receives the route request at time t_2, where $t_1 < t_2$. More recent location information for D may potentially be known by node I (as compared to node S), and the expected zone based on that information may be different from previous request zone Z. Therefore, request zone initially determined at a source node may be adapted at node I.

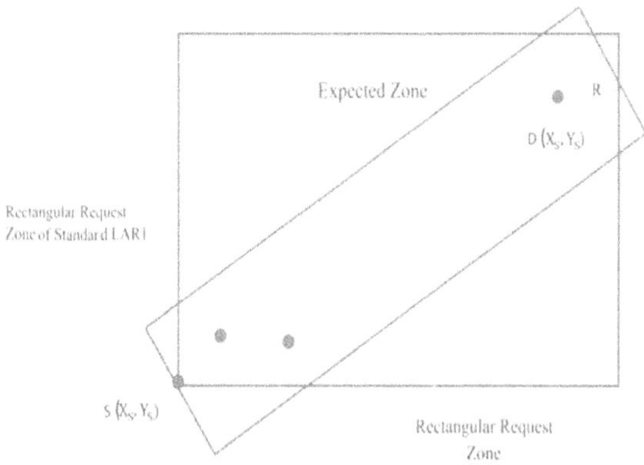

Figure 6.5: Tilted Rectangular Zone

For instance, when using LAR scheme 1, node I may determine the expected zone using more recent location information for node D, and define the adapted request zone as the smallest rectangle containing node S and the new expected zone for node D.

In this scheme, the source node S finds out the coordinates of the four request zone vertices. These coordinates are comparative to the plane where the node S is the origin and the x-axis is parallel to the line between S and D. After that, the source translates these coordinates (for the four vertices) to the real coordinates by means of this formula

$$x = x_1 \times \frac{(y_D - y_S)}{l} + y_1 \times \frac{x_D - x_S}{l} + x_S$$
$$y = x_1 \times \frac{(x_S - x_d)}{l} + y_1 \times \frac{y_D - y_S}{l} + y_S$$

Where (x_1, y_1) are the coordinates of the vertex in the initial plane, and I is the distance between the source node S and the destination node D. Therefore, the coordinates of the four vertices area measured. These coordinates are integrated in the route request packet when commencing the route discovery process. RREQ broadcast is limited to this rectangular request zone. Thus, a node, $I(x_1, y_1)$ forwards the RREQ packet barely when it is in the request zone:

$$\begin{cases} x_I \geq RequestZone.topLeft.x, and \\ x_I \leq RequestZone.bottomRight.x, and \\ y_I \geq RequestZone.bottomLeft.x, and \\ y_I \leq RequestZone.topRight.x \end{cases}$$

Therefore in this method the source node S includes the coordinates of the vertices of the request zone within the route request message.

6.4.1. Security Considerations

To ensure a secure routing algorithm against attacks, three main properties should be satisfied. Initially, nodes should be able to validate each other through the process of routes establishment. Datagrams generated with forged information should be redundant before reaching the destination mobile node called as MD. Secondly, every node should not be in position of generating and forwarding datagrams to MD, but also of controlling the behaviour of its neighbour. Also, watchdog method is used to identify nodes that do not forward the datagrams as estimated. A node which makes use of watchdog technique is able to decide whether its neighbour nodes are forwarding the datagram they receive or not. If the packet is not forwarded within a definite period, this neighbour is measured as malicious (Jain,S. and P.D.Chadda 2013). Every node should sustain two lists: a list of one-hop neighbours and a list of two hop neighbours.

The two lists are fashioned by hiring every node periodically perform a two-hop broadcast of a Hello Message (i.e., by setting the TTL equal to 2). A node, state as n1 which receives a generated Hello message by a node, say n0, with a TTL equal to 2, add the identity of n0 to its list of neighbours, appends it own identity (i.e., n1), decreases by one the TTL, and forwards the packet. A node, say n2, which receives a datagram with a TTL equal to 1 from the neighbour node n1, adds the identity of the sender (i.e., n0) to its list of two hop neighbours, and marks this node as life form reachable in the course of the immediate sender n1. Third, when a node detects a malicious neighbour, both the source and the destination nodes should be well-versed.

To protect the routing algorithm adjacent to forgery of false routing information, a signature based scheme is employed to authenticate nodes and guarantee the integrity of the information they exchange. Suppose, in case of WSN, every node joining the network is authenticated by the BS. Intermediate verification of packets signature permits to remove compromised packets before they reach the destination nodes, which optimizes the used energy and communication resources, and reduces the overhead of the signature verification process performed by the destination node. For the period of the routes establishment, every node generates or forwards the RReq, and adds its identity, the identity of the next receiving nodes, and sur-signs record the route. A node which may receiving the forwarded message confirm whether the final appended signature is correct or not, may checks if it is assumed destination, determines the immediate sender (the neighbour node from which the packet is being forwarded) of that datagram and makes sure that it is a neighbour. In case, it adds its identity, the identity of the feasible next hops and sur-signs the datagram.

As an alternative of WSN, signature is performed by means of elliptic threshold signature algorithm provided by (Razak, S.A., S.M.Furnell and P.J.Brooke, 2004) is used. It allows to generate a public key *kpub, n* associated with secret keys *kpr1 , ..., kprn*. Every signature produced by a private keys called as *kpri*, can be checked by *kpub*.Every node uses its own private key for signature, whereas the same public key is employed by all the other nodes for the purpose of signature verification. In general types of Adhoc networks, where nodes can enter and leave the network at any time perfid, and no resource limits may exist, normal signature can be used. Every node should contain its own private and public keys, where a certificate, containing this public key, is delivered by a certification authority. Mobiles nodes will employ the certificates of the senders to make sure the integrity of the signed datagrams.

Assume that each mobile node has the capacity to make contact with a certification authority depository to download the certificate of any node in the network. These techniques increase the flexibility to nodes compromise, particularly in the circumstance of WSN they protect against nodes confine. The protection is done by: (a) with digital signature to authenticate packet content and removal of invalid datagrams (b) with the identification of captured node based on applied watchdog mechanism and intermediate signature; and (c) authorizing *x* shared nodes in order to be liberal to discard of compromised paths involving captured node, which assures that, even when part of the nodes have been captured, the rest of the network remains secure.

In the context of WSN, where threshold signature is used, if a node is duplicated and its key is used via a malicious node, *MD* will observe the attack by detecting that the same key was used by several nodes. To carry out the process *MD* checks whether two nodes having the same identities have participated in forwarding the *RReq*. If it is not, for each signature adds to the *RReq*, the *MD* finds the identity of the signer node, and verifies whether it could really create this signature if its private key was used (in the case of WSNs the *MD*, which is the base station, is assumed to know all the mobile nodes private keys).

Note that the use of the public key is not enough to validate the nodes, because it does not permit to detect whether the same private key was used several times to generate the sur-signed *RReq*. When the *BS* detects that a node has used the private key of another node, or a node has participated numerous times in the similar *RReq*, it forwards an alert containing the identity of the compromised nodes, requesting for the remaining nodes in the network to reject any packet sent from that node in the future.

When a node receives a second copy of the *RReq*, it signs and stores the received path in the *RP* list, where each identity, in the received path, is signed by intermediate nodes. If a malicious node wants to modify the *RP* list, it must use the signatures of all nodes involved in the modified path to re-sign each identity which is impossible. In addition, when an intermediate node eliminates a received *RP* list instead of forwarding it, the watchdog mechanism used by neighbour nodes will detect such behavior.

6.4.2. *Experimental Results*

In order to evaluate the proposed method, the simulation is carried out using simulator version 2 (NS-2). Number of nodes in the network is selected to be 20, 30 and 50 for different simulation runs. The nodes are limited in a 1000x1000 m^2 area. Their primary locations are attained by means of a uniform distribution. Individual nodes move about next in a random waypoint mobility representation, each node moves incessantly, without pausing at any location.

The performance of the proposed method is evaluated by the following metrics.

i.   Packet delivery ratio (PDR): PDR is the ratio of the number of data packets received by the destination to the number of data packets sent by the source. This metric shows the reliability of data packet delivery. In figure 6.6, PDR is plotted against the number of nodes.

ii.   Packet overhead: The number of transmitted routing packets. For example, a

iii.   HELLO or TC message sent over four hops would be counted as four packets in this metric. In figure 6.7, packet overhead has been plotted against number of nodes.

iv.   Average delay: This metric represents average end-to-end and indicates how long it took for a packet to travel from the source to the application layer of the destination. It is measured in seconds.

v.   Throughput: This metric represents the total number of bits forwarded to higher layers per second. It is measured in bps. It can also be defined as the total amount of data a receiver actually receives to obtain the last packet.

The following table 6.1 compares the proposed RZLSR method with the existing SeMuRAMAS.

Table 6.1: Comparison Results

Observational Parameters	SeMuRAMAS			RZLSR		
No. of nodes	50	100	150	50	100	150
Generated Packets	132	71	91	182	78	122
Received Packets	120	51	81	171	72	115
Ratio	90.9	71.83	89.01	93.95	92.3	94.26
Dropped Packets	12	20	10	11	6	7
Routing Load	0.53	2.8	2.01	0.29	0.38	0.24
CBR Bytes	18224	88540	81228	7076	8480	11144
Route bytes	5252	12828	14816	3624	3008	3696
Route Costs	0.2	0.1	0.18	0.06	0.3	0.24

From the experimental results, it is observed that RZLSR scheme outperforms the SeMuRAMAS technique in terms of low route cost, reduced routing load, average CBR delay, lesser dropped packets and 20% improvement in delivery ratio when the rate is increased.

The Figure 6.6 illustrates the comparison of packet delivery ratio between SeMuRAMAS and RZLSR algorithms. It is observed that RZLSR algorithm performs better in terms of packet delivery ratio compared to SeMuRAMAS algorithm.

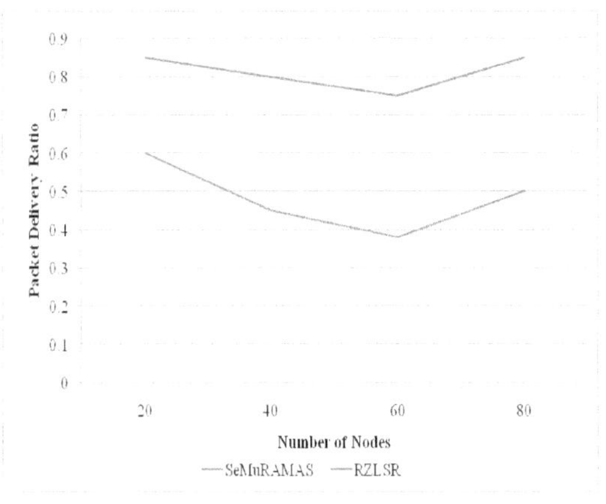

Figure 6.6: Packet Delivery Ratio vs. Number of Nodes

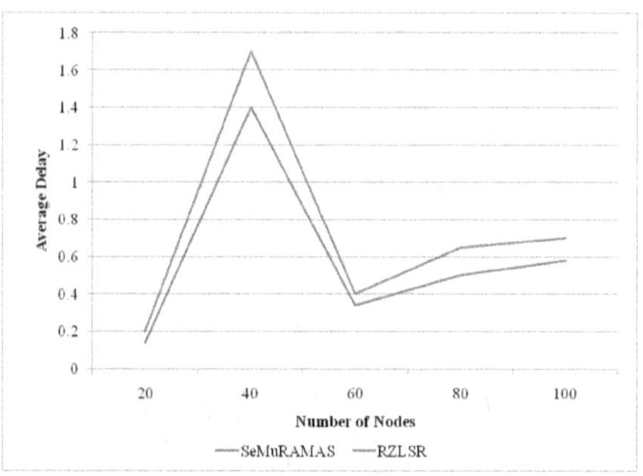

Figure 6.7: Average Delay vs. Number of Nodes

Figure 6.7 compares the average delay between SeMuRAMAS and RZLSR algorithms. It is observed from the result that the average delay is found high in SeMuRAMAS algorithm compared to RZLSR algorithm. Therefore, RZLSR algorithm performs better in average delay.

Figure 6.8 shows the comparison throughput between SeMuRAMAS and RZLSR algorithms.

It is observed from the result that RZLSR algorithm provides high throughput compared to SeMuRAMAS. The difference between the two algorithms is found high at less number of nodes. When the number of nodes increases, the throughput does not show significant difference between the performance of two algorithms.

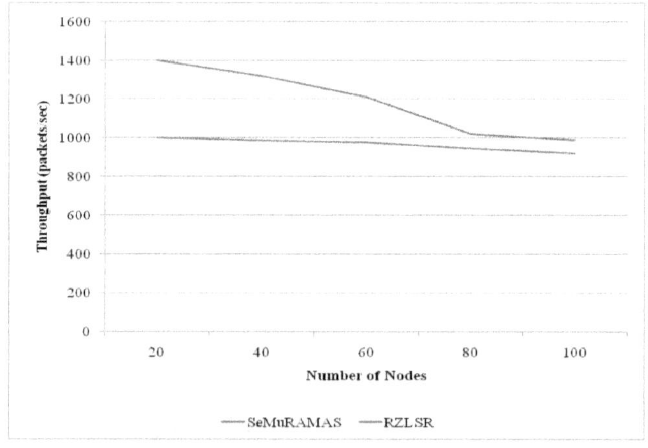

Figure 6.8: Throughput vs. Number of Nodes

Figure 6.9 shows the comparison of routing overhead between SeMuRAMAS and RZLSR algorithms. It is observed from the result that according to the increase in the number of nodes, the routing overhead also linearly increases. The comparative analysis depicts that RZLSR algorithm gives persistently better performance than SeMuRAMAS algorithm. The performance of RZLSR is found significant compared to SeMuRAMAS when the number of nodes crosses more than 80 nodes.

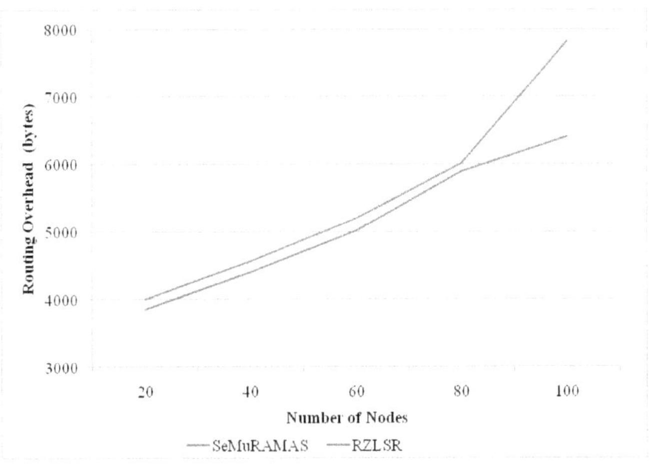

Figure 6.9: Routing Overhead vs. Number of Nodes

6.5.   Summary

Rectangular Zone based Location Specific Routing (RZLSR) method considers both areas of routing and bandwidth. At first, it provides more efficient routing method which improves the quality of services in terms of routing overhead. Secondly, it combines two concept of Location specific Routing to improve the route discovery process. SeMuRAMAS algorithm is considered as main point of comparison with the RZLSR. The performance of the proposed RZLSR algorithm has been analyzed. From the simulation results obtained, it is observed that the RZLSR algorithm optimizes the route discovery process thereby it reduces the routing overhead effectively.

CHAPTER 7

ADAPTIVE SECURE MULTIPATH ROUTING (ASMR)

Adaptive secure Multi-path routing (ASMR) mechanism, which allows nodes in MASNet to perform an on-demand discovery and generation of a set of paths has been designed and implemented. This new technique adopts Dynamic MPR (DMPR) protocol for route discovery process and the Quadrant based secured multipath routing protocol and Rectangular Zone based Location Specific Routing (RZLSR) protocol for route maintenance. The overall efficiency of the routing scheme has been improved by this method.

7.1. Introduction

The proposed methods for secure multipath routing namely DMPR, QRS, and RZLSR has been proved to be more efficient than the existing SeMuRAMAS algorithm. In order to optimize the new techniques to improve the overall performance of MASNet, a new secure multipath routing technique has been designed. The proposed DMPR algorithm uses improved multipoint relay method to propagate the route request to the selective range of mobile nodes. Further, this method is found more efficient than the other two proposed methods. Hence this method is adopted here in the route discovery phase. Due to dynamic nature of the mobile nodes, route failure may happen at any time. At this point, QRS or RZLSR algorithm speeds up the response time through location information and hence they are incorporated in this technique.

This proposed routing scheme improves the packet delivery ratio from source to destination since it provides the optimal path in terms of bandwidth, better quality of service, throughput and other related parameters. This approach provides a solution through restricted flooding thereby it reduces the power consumption.

7.2. Adaptive Secure Multipath Routing (ASMR)

A. Route Discovery Phase

This is the mechanism used when S wants to establish a set of paths with DM. Route Request datagrams, say RReq, are sent by S when it does not already have a route to DM. The entirely on-demand properties allow an Adaptive secure Multi-path routing(ASMR) to minimize the overhead and specify the path-disjointness threshold value. After receiving list of potential paths, S computes all paths to the destination which satisfy the specified threshold, chooses the list of paths to be used, caches the remaining ones, and starts sending the data.

Keeping information regarding unused paths allows the reaction to routes modification to be rapid and decreases the overhead related to the generation of a new RReq.

In Multipath DSR, generally HELLO message aids in discovering neighbours. It is send periodically by a node to determine its one-hop neighbours. They are generated and transmitted to all one-hop neighbours to achieve link-sensing, neighbour-sensing, two hop neighbour-sensing and MPR selector sensing. Two-hop HELLO message allows each node to maintain two up-to date lists, first list contains one-hop neighbours and second list contain 2-hop neighbours. Nodes in the network maintain list of all nodes that are reachable via symmetric neighbours in the routing table. It helps in MPR calculation. The nodes that have been selected as MPR are informed through HELLO message.

B. *Route Maintenance Phase*

In this phase, Adaptive secure Multi-path routing (ASMR) mechanism is proposed based on QRS and RZLSR protocol to reduce the link error and also to improve the network security. This is the mechanism used by intermediate nodes to let S update the list of paths in use when the network structure changes or some routes are broken down owing to an attack or sleeping cycles of nodes. This mechanism is based on letting middle nodes bring into play the watchdog concept for every packet and they forward to detect the identities of misbehaving nodes or detect routes errors. If the next hop appears to be broken down, a route error packet, say RErr, is generated and sent to S with the intention to decrease the number of possible path to the destination. The S will consider all the path as broken and endeavor to use another route that goes over the non-responding stored in its cache, which allows to maintain the DPRM. If none backup route to DM is in the cache, the source node invokes again the Route Discovery mechanism.

To endow with a secure routing algorithm, adjacent to a set of attacks, which plan for the study, were three main properties should be satisfied. Initially, nodes should be able to validate each other's through the process of routes establishment. Datagrams generated with forged information should be redundant before reaching the destination mobile node called as MD. Secondly, every node should not be in position of generating and forwarding datagrams to MD, but also of controlling the behavior of its neighbours. Also, the watchdog method is used to identify nodes that do not forward the datagrams as estimated. A node which makes use of watchdog technique is able to decide whether its neighbour nodes are forwarding the datagram they receive or not.

If the packet is not forwarded within a definite period, this neighbour is measured as malicious. Every node should sustain two lists: a list of one-hop neighbours and a list of two hop neighbours.

The two lists are fashioned by hiring every node periodically perform a two-hop broadcast of a Hello Message (i.e., by setting the TTL equal to 2). A node, state as n1 which receives a generated Hello message by a node, say n0, with a TTL equal to 2, add the identity of n0 to its list of neighbors, appends it own identity (i.e., n1), decreases by one the TTL, and forwards the packet. A node, say n2, which receives a datagram with a TTL equal to 1 from the neighbor node n1, adds the identity of the sender (i.e., n0) to its list of two hop neighbors, and marks this node as life form reachable in the course of the immediate sender n1. Third, when a node detects a malicious neighbor, both the source and the destination nodes should be well-versed.

i. *QUAD based Adaptive Secured Multipath Routing Protocol (ASMR) for Route Maintenance*

The proposed routing algorithm imposes the route discovery process and maintenance in conjunction with LAR [14] and ASMR. Six kinds of datagram are used by QUAD throughout the route discovery in [13]. The function of LAR in QUAD implants the location information and timestamp of each node to its neighbours. In that way source node can identify the location of destination node regarding the route cache. LAR with directional antenna can reduce the routing overhead and recommend effectiveness. The general thing is considered here which has found less influence on conventional method. By this way, QUAD scheme is used to reduce the broadcast region and speedy the process of path establishment.

The above proposed algorithm illustrates that network range can be noted from the density of nodes in the network. As a result, it is essential to identify the center point and radius of the network space. The next step involves in slicing the network space based on the availability of information into quadruple format and assigns the region label. Algorithm now triggered to assess the belongingness of SN and DN node's region. If both SN_region and DN_region are same, it returns the Lm_region as SN_region therefore the original broadcasting range is limited to the specific range.

Or else, SN_region and DN_region are compared as adjacent region in either way. If both are adjacent, now the Lm_region trying to merge the SN_region and DN_region and return the Lm_region as limited network space. If the preceding conditions fail, it means that SN_region and DN_region are belongs to opposite direction. Hence, this sequence is not advised to merge; because the center portion of the merging effect will be narrow band. In this situation, the chances of communication between inter-region nodes are nearly impossible. Thus, intermediate region should be formed to avoid such kind of problems. In this case, we have two intermediate regions and the selection of appropriate region is measured in terms of distance function between neighbouring region and DN. Less distance indicates the closeness to the intermediate region. Therefore, SN_region, Im_region and DN_region are merged together as single limited network space.

```
QUAD LNS Algorithm
   // Limiting Network Space through QUAD broadcasting scheme QUAD_LNS
   (Network Space, SN, DN)
   {Find center point of the network space and radius;
        Classify the network space into quad format Ql,Q2,Q3,Q4; Evaluate the
        region of source and destination nodes;
        If (SN_Region = DN_Region)
        {// Limiting the network region Lm_Region  =
        SN_Region; Return the Lm_Region;}
   // if SN_Region is adjacent to DN_Region either way Else if(SN_edge
   = DN_edge)
   {//Merging of selected regions
        Lm_Region  =  SN_Region  +  DN  Region;  Return  the
        Lm_Region;}
   Else
   { Predict the distance of DN from two adjacent quads of SN;
        // Intermediate Region
        Im_Region = Region has Less distance to DN;
        //Merging of selected regions
        Lm_Region = SN_Region + DN_Region + Im_Region; } }
```

ii. *Rectangular Zone based Location Specific Routing (RZLSR) Approach for Route Maintenance*

The rectangular shaped request zone is only implemented. For example, it is feasible to remove the available restriction when defining the rectangular region: one side of the rectangle may be made parallel to the line connecting the location of source node S to the previous location of D in figure 7.1.

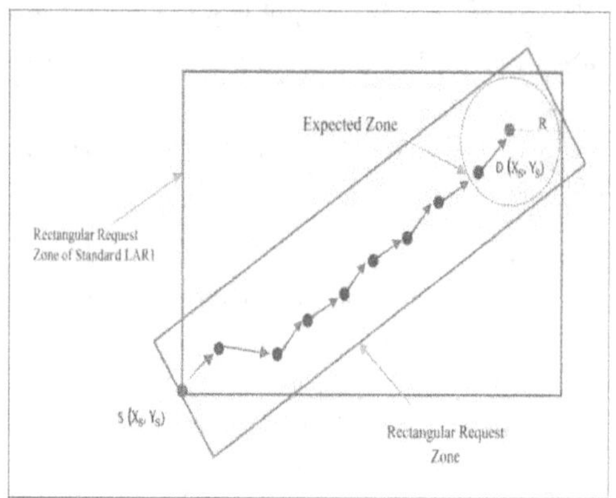

Figure 7.1: Alternative Definitions of Request Zone: Tilted Rectangular Shaped

In this scheme, the source node S finds out the coordinates of the four request zone vertices. These coordinates are comparative to the plane where the node S is the origin and the x-axis is parallel to the line between S and D. After that, the source translates these coordinates (for the four vertices) to the real coordinates by means of this formula

$$x = x_1 \times \frac{(y_D - y_S)}{l} + y_1 \times \frac{x_D - x_S}{l} + x_S$$

$$y = x_1 \times \frac{(x_S - x_d)}{l} + y_1 \times \frac{y_D - y_S}{l} + y_S$$

Where (x_I, y_I) are the coordinates of the vertex in the initial plane, and I is the distance between the source node S and the destination node D. Therefore, the coordinates of the four vertices area measured. These coordinates are integrated in the route request packet when commencing the route discovery process. RREQ broadcast is limited to this rectangular request zone. Thus, a node, $I(x_I, y_I)$ forwards the RREQ packet barely when it is in the request zone:

$$\begin{cases} x_I \geq RequestZone.topLeft.x, and \\ x_I \leq RequestZone.bottomRight.x, and \\ y_I \geq RequestZone.bottomLeft.x, and \\ y_I \leq RequestZone.topRight.x \end{cases}$$

Therefore in RZLSR method called (titled rectangular shaped) where the source node S includes the coordinates of the vertices of the request zone within the route request message. To protect the routing algorithm adjacent to forgery of false routing information, a signature based scheme is employed to authenticate nodes and guarantee the integrity of the information they exchange. Suppose, in case of WSN, every node joining the network is authenticated by the BS. Intermediate verification of packets signature permits to remove compromised packets before they reach the destination nodes, which optimizes the used energy and communication resources, and reduces the overhead of the signature verification process performed by the destination node. For the period of the routes establishment, every node generates or forwards the RReq, and adds its identity, the identity of the next receiving nodes, and sur-signs record the route. A node which may receiving the forwarded message confirm whether the final appended signature is correct or not, may checks if it is assumed destination, determines the immediate sender (the neighbour node from which the packet is being forwarded) of that datagram and makes sure that it is a neighbour. In case, it adds its identity, the identity of the feasible next hops and sur-signs the datagram. As an alternative of WSN, signature is performed by means of elliptic threshold signature algorithm is used. In addition, when an intermediate node eliminates a received *RP* list instead of forwarding it, the watchdog mechanism used by neighbour nodes will detect such behavior.

7.3.   Experimental Results

In order to evaluate the proposed protocol, the simulation is carried out using simulator version 2 (NS-2). NS-2 is a famous network simulation tool. Number of nodes in the network is selected to be 20, 30 and 50 for different simulation runs. The nodes are limited in a 1000x1000 m^2 area. Their primary locations are attained by means of a uniform distribution. Individual nodes move about next in a random waypoint mobility representation as there in each node moves incessantly, without pausing at any location.

Table 7.1: Simulation Parameters

Parameters	Value
Transmission Range	250
Bandwidth (Mbps)	512
Max. node speed (m sec^{-1})	7
Pause time (sec)	0
Packet size (Kb)	1000
Average TTL (sec)	40
No. of data items	1000
Traffic	CBR
Simulation time (sec)	20

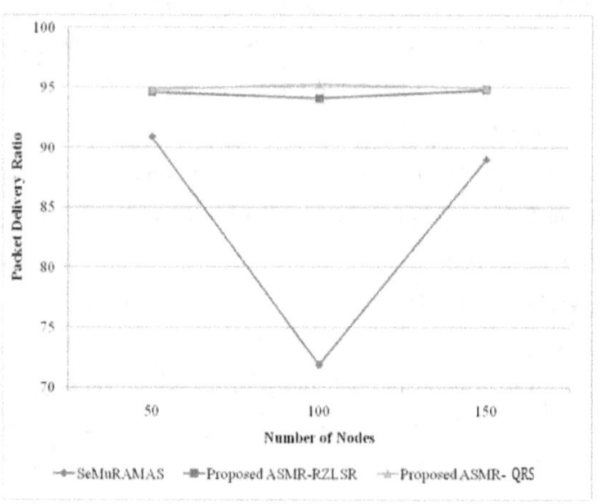

Figure 7.2: Packet Delivery Ratio

The figure 7.2 shows the comparison of packet delivery ratio values between SeMuRAMAS, ASMR-QRS and ASMR-RZLSR. It is observed from the result that ASMR-QRS and ASMR-RZLSR algorithms are outperforming than SeMuRAMAS algorithm. According to packet delivery ratio, the ASMR-QRS performance is slightly better than ASMR-RZLSR. The proposed algorithms are found to have significant impact on packet delivery ratio.

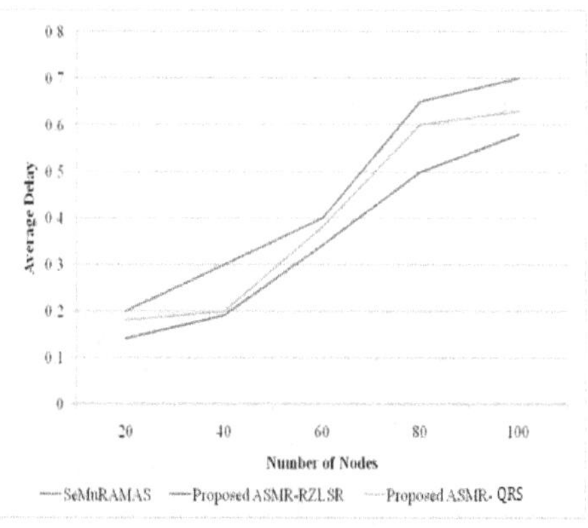

Figure 7.3: Average Delay

Figure 7.3 illustrates the comparison of average delay between SeMuRAMAS, ASMR-QRS and ASMR-RZLSR algorithms. It is observed from the graph that ASMR-RZLSR proposal is more efficient in terms of very less average delay time, than SeMuRAMAS and ASMR-QRS algorithms.

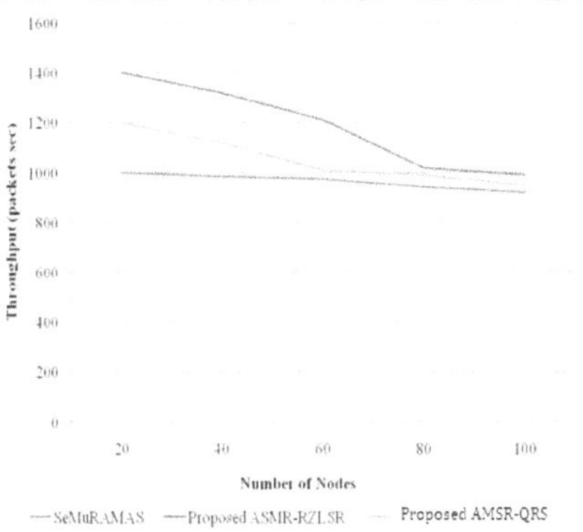

Figure 7.4: Throughput

The Figure 7.4 illustrates throughput versus number of nodes for the proposed and existing method. From the figure, it is observed that the proposed ASMR-RZLSR system has high throughput value when compared with ASMR-QRS scheme and SeMuRAMAS.

Figure 7.5 shows Routing Overhead Vs Number of nodes. From the figure it is observed that the proposed ASMR-RZLSR system has low Routing Overhead value compared with ASMR-QRS scheme and SeMuRAMAS.

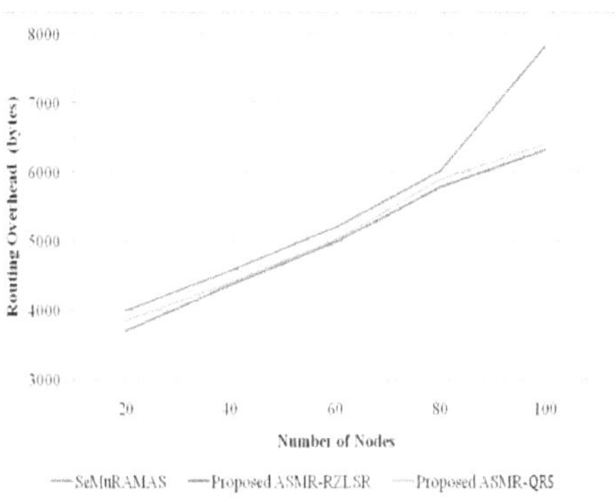

Figure 7.5: Routing Overhead

7.4.　Summary

An Adaptive Secure Multipath Routing Algorithm (ASMR) is developed for Mobile Ad-hoc and Sensor Networks to make secure route discovery. The experimental results show that the performance of ASMR-RZLSR is better than ASMR-QRS.

CHAPTER 8

PERFORMANCE EVALUATION

The performances of the proposed methods are evaluated by the following metrics.

- **Packet Delivery Ratio (PDR):** It is the ratio of number of packets received to that of number of packets send. If this rate is high then reliability of network is high.
- **Routing Load:** It is the ratio of number of routing packets sends to that of number of data packets received. If routing load is high then throughput of the network is low.
- **CBR Bytes:** Total size of data packets in bytes received at the destination.
- **Route bytes:** Total size of control packets in bytes transmitted by source and intermediate node.
- **Route cost:** It is defined as the ratio of Route bytes to that of CBR byte.

Table 8.1: Simulated Data

Nodes	Simulation Setup	SeMuR-AMAS	DMPR	QUAD	RZLSR	ASMR(QRS)	ASMR(RZLSR))
50	PDR	90.90	96.06	94.5	93.95	95.01	94.61
	Routing Load	0.53	0.16	0.34	0.29	0.30	0.18
	Route Costs	0.04	0.01	0.28	0.06	0.24	0.02
100	PDR	71.83	85.71	96.06	92.30	96.07	96.05
	Routing Load	2.86	0.93	1.07	0.84	0.98	0.89
	Route Costs	0.25	0.19	0.56	0.38	0.49	0.16
150	PDR	89.01	95.00	96.06	94.26	95.07	94.78
	Routing Load	2.01	0.91	0.97	0.76	0.78	0.65
	Route Costs	0.18	0.17	0.63	0.24	0.56	0.17

The results obtained from the experiments under different network size such as 50, 100& 150 nodes tested in NS-2 simulation environment are listed in Table 8.1. The performances of the proposed schemes are compared with the existing SeMuRAMAS.

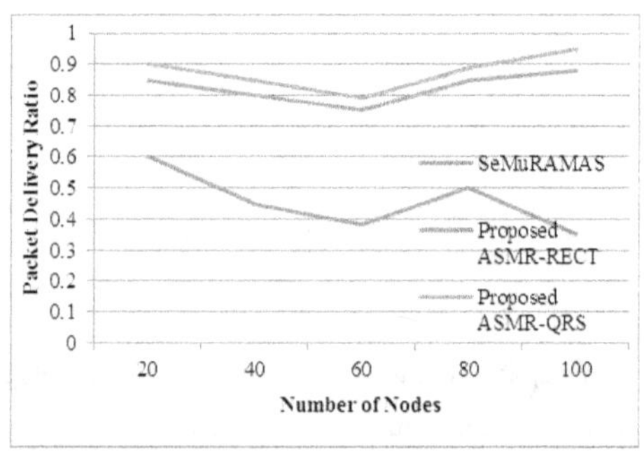

Figure 8.1: Packet Delivery Vs Number of Nodes

The results show that ASMR-QRS system has high packet delivery ratio when compared with ASMR-RZLSR scheme and the existing SeMuRAMAS technique. From the graph (Figure 8.1) between packet delivery and Number of nodes, it is observed that the proposed ASMR-RZLSR and ASMR-QRS are more efficient on packet delivery ratio compared to SeMuRAMAS.

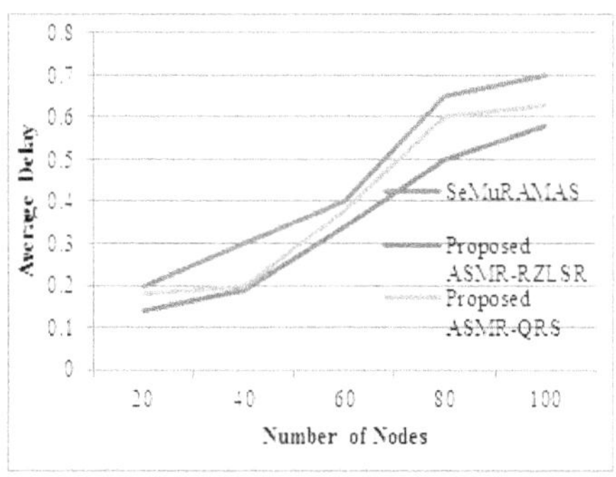

Figure 8.2: Average Delay Vs Number of Nodes

The graph (Figure 8.2) between Average Delay and Number of nodes shows that ASMR-RZLSR scheme has low Average Delay when compared with ASMR-QRS scheme and SeMuRAMAS.

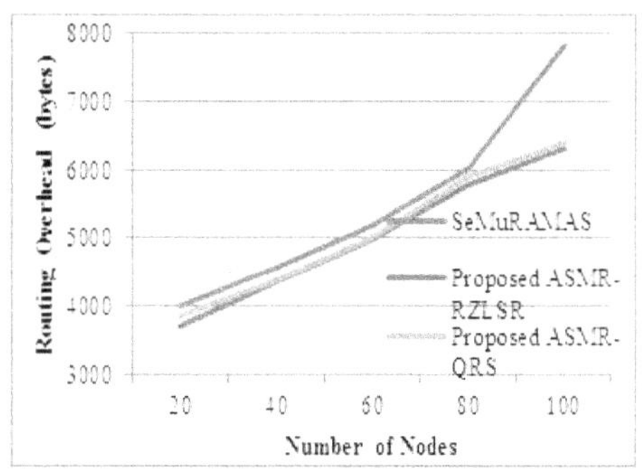

Figure 8.3: Routing Overhead Vs Number of Nodes

Also the graph (Figure 8.3) between the Routing Overhead and Number of nodes result shows that ASMR-RZLSR system has low Routing Overhead value when compared with ASMR-QRS scheme and SeMuRAMAS. The results depicts that the proposed Adaptive Secure Multipath Routing scheme generates low routing load, low route cost and increases packet delivery ratio than existing scheme under all scenario.

CHAPTER 9

CONCLUSION AND SCOPE FOR FUTURE WORK

9.1. Conclusion

Mobile ad-hoc network (MANET) is a collection of self configuring mobile nodes interconnected through wireless connections. Wireless sensor network (WSN) consists of thousands of low cost nodes with limited energy, computing power and communication capabilities. In general, MANET and WSN are sharing the similar idea on routing scheme. This research work is mainly constructed on two special parameters, namely security and multipath routing provision. Security is considered to be the most important factor for reliability of data and transmission. Further, security constraints are estimated through various attributes such as availability, confidentiality, integrity, authentication, non-reputation. Multipath routing is an effective strategy to utilize the resources for providing a pathway when an unexpected failure happens. Therefore, the multipath routing technique increases the chances quality of services in the MANET and WSN environment.

The Secure multipath routing algorithm for mobile ad hoc and sensor networks (SeMuRAMAS) is an extension of Dynamic Source Routing (DSR) algorithm. SeMURAMAS is a recent proposal by Bayrem Triki (2012), which combines the security and multipath routing techniques in MASNET environment. It perform an on-demand discovery and generation of a set of paths, while specifying a disjointness threshold, representing the maximal number of nodes shared between any two paths in the set of the k established paths. SeMuRAMAS is adaptive, secure, and uses labels to carry the disjointness-threshold between nodes during the route discovery. A set of security mechanisms, based on the use of Watchdog and digital signature, are used to protect the route discovery process.

In this research work, a few areas in SeMuRAMAS algorithm have been identified for improvement. The following are the observations made in the existing method. (1) When a mobile node joins the network; it broadcasts a two hop HELLO message. Therefore each node is required to maintain two up-to-date lists. The first list denotes the list of neighbours and the second one denotes the neighbours of each neighbour. (2) The disjointness threshold is set by the sender to specify the maximum number of nodes that could be shared by any two paths among the set of paths to establish with the destination node. (3) The scheme broadcasts the RREQ to all nodes in the networks and insists to store the information regardless of possible routes between source and destination. (4) In SeMuRAMAS the network overload will increase depending up on the number of nodes and the value of the threshold x. In majority of the situations the increase of overhead is unavoidable. (5) High number of lists of paths may be generated which it influences to increase the number of datagrams.

In this work, four new proposals which are mainly targeted towards the impact of restricted broadcasting sequence have been presented. The Dynamic MPR (DMPR)uses an enhancement on multipoint relay technique. The DMPR algorithm effectively restricts the broadcasting area; thereby it reduces the route discovery process timing and the experiment result also depicts the same. The DMPR algorithm performs well in terms of routing overhead, routing cost and packet delivery ratio.

The QRS uses quadrant feature in association with LAR protocol to optimize the route discovery timing.

LAR protocol is a location aided routing protocol which uses location information to reduce the search space for a desired route and limiting the search space results in fewer route discovery messages. Compared to SeMuRAMAS algorithm, QRS algorithm performs better in terms of route discovery phase. LAR is used to embed the location information in the routing packet. Further, the QRS scheme is applied to reduce the network space by QUAD_LNS sequence between source and destination nodes. The performance evaluation between SeMuRAMAS and QRS confirms the QRS routing is performing better. The original effect on QRS is not achieved due to existing procedures of SeMuRAMAS, hence future work should address on threshold value and reduce the overheads.

The RZLSR algorithm uses tilted rectangular region feature for enhancement. RZLSR algorithm proposed is an extension of LAR protocol with tilted rectangle shape. The main advantage of this method is to optimize the route discovery process thereby reduces the routing overhead effectively and have energy efficient. The ASMR combines DMPR with QRS and RZLSR sequences. Since, the DMPR technique is identified as typical technique to improve the route discovery process it is estimated as an energy efficient method. The QRS and RZLSR algorithms can react more quickly than DMPR algorithm. Therefore, QRS and RZLSR algorithms are efficient when network failure happens. Further, this technique is very much useful on the route maintenance phase. The ASMR algorithm combines the power of DMPR with QRS and RZLSR. The experimental result shows that in majority of the cases ASMR-RZLSR out performs ASMR-QRS.

The research work contributes design and development of routing four efficient routing algorithms in Mobile Ad-hoc and Sensor Networks. The Dynamic Multipath Routing scheme incorporates threshold based multipath routing which reduces the routing overhead. The Quadrant Based Routing scheme reduces or limits the network space to selected regions and the incorporation of LAR further reduces the routing overhead. In the rectangular Zone Based Location Specific Routing scheme, the area of the request zone is reduced optimally based on the location and distance of the expected zone. The Adaptive Secure Multipath Routing (ASMR) scheme which incorporates the above three techniques is efficient in allowing nodes in MASNet to perform on demand route discovery and generation of optimal path. The performance evaluation confirms that the proposed routing algorithms are efficient in reducing the broadcasting range, network routing load and route cost.

9.2.   Scope for Future Research

This research has put enormous effort to exhibit the impact of broadcasting sequences in the route discovery and route maintenance phase on MASNET environment.

- The future research can separately examine the effect of broadcasting sequences with MANET and WSN. Since, MANET and WSN environments are not exactly same. Hence, this kind of investigation will provide more insights and exhibit the true performance indication.

- The future research also can examine the effect of change in security features considered in this research. The Watchdog mechanism and digital signature provides the essential security for MASNET environment. Isolated evaluation of security mechanism can exhibit the adaptability of security technique in a particular environment.

References

1. Wei, W., and Zakhor, A., "Robust multipath source routing protocol (RMPSR) for video communication over wireless ad hoc networks", IEEE international conference on multimedia and expo, Vol.2, Pp. 1379-1382, 2004.

2. Qayyum, A., Viennot, L., and Laouiti, A., "Multipoint relaying for flooding broadcast messages in mobile wireless networks", Proceedings of the 35th Annual Hawaii International Conference on System Sciences (HICSS'02), Vol.9, Pp. 298, 2002.

3. Abduvaliyev, A., Pathan, A. S. K., Zhou, J., Roman, R., and Wong, W.C., "On the Vital Areas of Intrusion Detection Systems in Wireless Sensor Networks", IEEE Communications Surveys and Tutorials, Vol.15, No.3, Pp.1223-1237, 2013.

4. Agrawal, C.P., Vyas, O.P., and Udaykumar, P., "Analysis of MANET Security Challenges, Threats&Solutions", International Journal of Computer Science and Applications, Vol.3, No.1, 2010.

5. An, H.Y, Zhong L, Lu X.C, and Peng W., "A cluster-based multipath dynamic source routing in MANET", IEEE International Conference on Wireless and Mobile Computing, Networking and Communications (WIMOB), Vol.3, Pp. 369–76, 2005.

6. Ankita, V. N., SEAD AND ARIANE Routing Protocol: Comparative Study, 2014.

7. Aydip Sen, J., "Security and Privacy Issues in Wireless Mesh Networks: A Survey", Wireless Networks and Security: Issues, Challenges and Research Trends, 189, 2013.

8. Williams, B., and Camp, T., "Comparison of Broadcasting Techniques for Mobile Ad Hoc Networks", Proc. MOBIHOC, Pp. 194-205, 2002.

9. Blywis, B., Günes, M., Juraschek, F., Hahm, O., and Schmittberger, N., "A Survey of Flooding, Gossip Routing, and Related Schemes for Wireless Multi-Hop Networks", Technical Report TR-NO: TR-B-11-06, 2011.

10. Triki, B., Rekhis, S., and Boudriga, N., "Threshold Based Multipath Routing Algorithm in Mobile Adhoc and Sensor Networks", E-Business and Telecommunications, Pp.54-70, 2012.

11. Berton, S., Yin, H., Lin, C., and Min, G., "Secure, disjoint, multipath source routing protocol (SDMSR) for mobile ad-hoc networks", Fifth International Conference Grid and Cooperative Computing, Pp. 387-394, 2006.

12. Bing, H. L. H. F. P., and Jing, C. H. E. N., "Defend against Wormhole Attack Based on Neighbor Trust Evaluation in MANET", Computer Science, Vol. 8, p.035, 2006.

13. Vaidya, B., Makrakis, D., Park, J.H., and Yeo, S.S., "Resilient security mechanism for wireless ad hoc network", Wireless Personal Communications, Vol.56, No.3, Pp.385-401, 2011.

14. Biswal, S., Mohanty, S., and Seth, D., "Study of DSR Routing protocol in Mobile Adhoc network", International Conference on Information and Network Technology, 2011.

15. Bogdanoski, M., Suminoski, T., and Risteski, A., "Analysis of the SYN Flood DoS Attack", International Journal of Computer Network and Information Security (IJCNIS), Vol.5, No.8, Pp.1-11, 2013.

16. Bouam, S., and Ben-Othman, J., "Data security in ad hoc networks using multipath routing", 14th IEEE Proceedings on Personal, Indoor and Mobile Radio Communications, Vol. 2, Pp. 1331-1335, 2003.

17. Carzaniga, A., Rutherford, M.J., and Wolf, A.L., "A routing scheme for content-based networking", Twenty-third Annual Joint Conference of the IEEE Computer and Communications Societies(INFOCOM), Vol. 2, Pp. 918-928, 2004.

18. Chai, Z., Cao, Z., and Lu, R., "Threshold password authentication against guessing attacks in Ad hoc networks", Ad Hoc Networks, Vol.5, No.7, Pp.1046-1054, 2007.

19. Chandrakant, N., "Achieving MANETs Security by Exchanging Path Oriented Keys and Priority Based Secured Route Discovery", International Journal of Innovation and Applied Studies, Vol.5, No.3, Pp.294-300, 2014.

20. Chandrakant, N., "Invalidating Security Compromised Nodes by Releasing its Energy in MANETs", Proceedings of the Third International Conference on Soft Computing for Problem Solving, Springer, Pp. 247-257, 2014.

21. Chang, T.Y., Yang, C.C., and Hwang, M.S, "A threshold signature scheme for group communications without a shared distribution center", Future Generation Computer Systems, Vol.20, No.6, Pp.1013-1021, 2004.

22. Chen, H., Wu, H., Cao, X., and Gao, C., "Trust propagation and aggregation in wireless sensor networks", Japan-China Joint Workshop on Frontier of Computer Science and Technology, Pp. 13-20, 2007.

23. Chen, H., Wu, H., Hu, J., and Gao, C., "Agent-based trust management model for wireless sensor networks", International Conference on Multimedia and Ubiquitous Engineering, Pp. 150-154, 2008.

24. Chen, Y., Zhang, S., Xu, S., and Li, G.Y., "Fundamental trade-offs on green wireless networks", Communications Magazine, Vol.49, No.6, Pp.30-37, 2011.

25. Choksi, S., and Gondaliya, N.N., "Trust Based Routing Protocols for Mobile Ad Hoc Networks: A Survey", International Journal of Research in Advent Technology, 2014.

26. Conti, M., Maselli, G., Turi, G., and Giordano, S., "Cross-layering in mobile ad hoc network design", Computer, Vol.37, No.2, Pp.48-51, 2004.

27. Da Silva, A.P.R., Martins, M.H., Rocha, B.P., Loureiro, A.A., Ruiz, L.B., and Wong, H.C., "Decentralized intrusion detection in wireless sensor networks", 1st ACM international workshop on Quality of service & security in wireless and mobile networks, Pp. 16-23, 2005.

28. Das, T., Implementation of Capability Aware Routing Algorithm in NS-2 Environment, Doctoral dissertation, Jadavpur University Kolkata, 2010.

29. De, S., Qiao, C., and Wu, H., "Meshed multipath routing with selective forwarding: an efficient strategy in wireless sensor networks", Computer Networks, Vol.43, No.4, Pp.481-497, 2003.

30. Desmedt, Y., "Threshold cryptosystems", International Workshop on the Theory and Application of Cryptographic Techniques, Pp. 1-14, 1993.

31. D'Souza, R.J., & Varaprasad, G., "Digital signature-based secure node disjoint multipath routing protocol for wireless sensor networks", IEEE Sensors Journal, Vol.12, No.10, Pp.2941-2949, 2012.

32. Dubey, R., Jain, V., Thakur, R., and Choubey, S., "Attacks in wireless sensor networks", International Journal of Scientific & Engineering Research, Vol.3, No.3, 2012.

33. Engoulou, R.G., Bellaïche, M., Pierre, S., and Quintero, A., "VANET security surveys", Computer Communications, 44, Pp.1-13, 2014.

34. Ferri, R., Kim, M., & Yee, E. (2004).U.S. Patent Application 10/856,684.

35. Framework, U. A Weight Based Synchronization Detection for Wormhole Attack Using Periodic.

36. Gadallah, Y., and Serhani, M.A., "A WSN-driven service discovery technique for disaster recovery using mobile ad hoc networks", IEEE Wireless Days (WD), Pp. 1-5, 2011.

37. Geng, X., and Whinston, A.B., "Defeating distributed denial of service attacks", IT Professional, Vol.2, No.4, Pp.36-42, 2000.

38. Glynos, D., Kotzanikolaou, P., and Douligeris, C., "Preventing impersonation attacks in MANET with multi-factor authentication", Third International Symposium on Modeling and Optimization in Mobile, Ad Hoc, and Wireless Networks, Pp. 59-64, 2005.

39. Gomez, J., and Garcia-Macias, J.A., "MANET and WSN: Are they alike?", In International Conference on Parallel Processing Workshop, Pp. 1-20, 2005.

40. Guo, X.F., Chen, Y.Q., and Chen, G.H., "An aggregated multipath routing scheme for ad hoc networks", Journal of Software, Vol.15, No.4, Pp.594-603, 2004.

41. Haas, Z.J., "A new routing protocol for the reconfigurable wireless networks", International Conference on Universal Personal Communications Record, Vol. 2, Pp.562-566, 1997.

42. Han, G., Jiang, J., Shu, L., Niu, J., and Chao, H.C., "Management and applications of trust in Wireless Sensor Networks: A survey", Journal of Computer and System Sciences, Vol.80, No.3, Pp.602-617, 2014.

43. Han, H., Shakkottai, S., Hollot, C.V., Srikant, R., and Towsley, D., "Multi-path tcp: a joint congestion control and routing scheme to exploit path diversity in the internet", IEEE/ACM Transactions on Networking (TON), Vol.14, No.6, Pp.1260-1271, 2006.

44. Hua, K.A., and Sheu, S., "Skyscraper broadcasting: a new broadcasting scheme for metropolitan video-on-demand systems", ACM SIGCOMM Computer Communication Review, Vol.27, No.4, Pp. 89-100, 1997.

45. Huang, D., Wang, H., Huang, L., and Dai, Y., "Dynamic threshold secret sharing scheme", Journal-TSINGHUA University, Vol.46, No.1, 102, 2006.

46. Huang, L., and Liu, L., "Extended watchdog mechanism for wireless sensor networks", Journal of Information and Computing Science, Vol.3, No.1, Pp.39-48, 2008.

47. Hussain, K., Abdullah, A.H., Awan, K.M., Ahsan, F., and Hussain, A., "Cluster head election schemes for WSN and MANET: a survey", World Applied Sciences Journal, Vol.23, No.5, Pp.611-620, 2013.

48. Wu, J., and Dai, F., "A Generic Distributed Broadcast Scheme in Ad Hoc Wireless Networks", IEEE Trans. Computers, Vol. 53, Pp. 1343–54, 2004

49. Jaisankar, N., and Saravanan, R., (2010). An extended AODV protocol for multipath routing in MANETs. IACSIT International Journal of Engineering and Technology,2(4), 394-400.

50. Jaisankar, N., Saravanan, R., and Swamy, K.D., "A novel security approach for detecting black hole attack in MANET", In Information Processing and Management, Springer Berlin Heidelberg, Pp. 217-223, 2010.

51. Jhaveri, R.H., Patel, S.J., and Jinwala, D.C., "A novel approach for grayhole and blackhole attacks in mobile ad hoc networks", 2012 Second International Conference on Advanced Computing & Communication Technologies (ACCT), Pp. 556-560, 2012.

52. Juhn, L.S., and Tseng, L.M., "Fast broadcasting for hot video access", Fourth International Workshop on Real-Time Computing Systems and Applications, Pp. 237-243, 1997.

53. Karlof, C., and Wagner, D., "Secure routing in wireless sensor networks: Attacks and countermeasures", Ad hoc networks, Vol.1, No.2, Pp.293-315, 2003.

54. Kaur, G., and Dhanda, E.S.K., "Analysing the effect of Wormhole Attack on Routing Protocol in Wireless Sensor Network", International Journal of Advanced Research in Computer and Communication Engineering, Vol.2, No.8, Pp.3217-3223, 2013.

55. Kong, J., Cui, J.H., Wu, D., and Gerla, M., "Building underwater ad-hoc networks and sensor networks for large scale real-time aquatic applications", IEEE Military Communications Conference, MILCOM, Pp. 1535-1541, 2005.

56. Kotzanikolaou, P., Mavropodi, R., and Douligeris, C., "Secure multipath routing for mobile ad hoc networks", Second Annual Conference on Wireless On-demand Network Systems and Services (WONS), Pp. 89-96, 2005.

57. Kozlov, D., Veijalainen, J., and Ali, Y., "Security and privacy threats in IoT architectures", Proceedings of the 7th International Conference on Body Area Networks. ICST (Institute for Computer Sciences, Social-Informatics and Telecommunications Engineering), Pp. 256-262, 2012.

58. Krishna, A.V., "Study of the effects of Noise on a New Model Based encryption Mechanism With time stamp and Acknowledgement support in MANET & WSN environment", International Journal of Advancements in Technology, Vol.2, No.1, Pp.14-21, 2011.

59. Kumar, P.S., Raghavaiah, B., and Babu, N.S., Design & implementation of teacher student interaction system using zigbee & rfid.

60. Lada Jr, H.F. (2000).U.S. Patent No. 6,041,416. Washington, DC: U.S. Patent and Trademark Office

61. Lazos, L., and Poovendran, R., "SeRLoc: Secure range-independent localization for wireless sensor networks", Proceedings of the 3rd ACM workshop on Wireless security, Pp. 21-30, 2004.

62. Lazos, L., Poovendran, R., and Čapkun, S., "ROPE: robust position estimation in wireless sensor networks", Proceedings of the 4th international symposium on Information processing in sensor networks, Pp. 43, 2005.

63. Lee, S.J, and Gerla, M., "SMR: split multipath routing with maximally disjoint paths in ad hoc networks", IEEE International Conference on communication, Vol.10, Pp.3201 – 3205, 2001.

64. Lee, B., Bae, S., and Han, D., "Design of network management platform and security framework for WSN", IEEE International Conference on Signal Image Technology and Internet Based Systems SITIS'08, Pp. 640-645, 2008.

65. Lee, J.W., Lee, Y.H., and Syrotiuk, V.R., "The performance of a watchdog protocol for wireless network security", International Journal of Wireless and Mobile Computing, Vol.2, No.1, Pp.28-36, 2007.

66. Liang, G., Agarwal, R., and Vaidya, N., "When watchdog meets coding", Proceedings IEEE INFOCOM, Pp. 1-9, 2010.

67. Lin, C.R., and Gerla, M., "Adaptive clustering for mobile wireless networks", IEEE Journal on Selected Areas in Communications, Vol.15, No.7, Pp.1265-1275, 1997.

68. Maquelin, O., Gao, G.R., Hum, H.H., Theobald, K.B., and Tian, X.M., "Polling watchdog: Combining polling and interrupts for efficient message handling", ACM SIGARCH Computer Architecture News, Vol. 24, No. 2, Pp.179-188, 1996.

69. Mavropodi, R., Kotzanikolaou, P., and Douligeris, C., "SecMR–a secure multipath routing protocol for ad hoc networks", Ad Hoc Networks, Vol.5, No.1, Pp.87-99, 2007.

70. Millberg, M., Nilsson, E., Thid, R., Kumar, S., and Jantsch, A., "The Nostrum backbone-a communication protocol stack for networks on chip", 17th International Conference on VLSI Design, Pp. 693-696, 2004.

71. Mirkovic, J., and Reiher, P., "A taxonomy of DDoS attack and DDoS defense mechanisms", ACM SIGCOMM Computer Communication Review, Vol.34, No.2, Pp.39-53, 2004.

72. Mishra, A.K., and Sahoo, B., "A modified Adaptive-SAODV prototype for performance enhancement in MANET", 2009.

73. Modirkhazeni, A., Aghamahmoodi, S., and Niknejad, N., "Distributed approach to mitigate wormhole attack in wireless sensor networks", The 7th International Conference on Networked Computing (INC), Pp. 122-128, 2011.

74. Momani, M., Challa, S., and Aboura, K., "Modelling trust in wireless sensor networks from the sensor reliability prospective", Innovative Algorithms and Techniques in Automation, Industrial Electronics and Telecommunications, Pp. 317-321, 2007.

75. Murphy, A.L., and Picco, G.P., "Transiently shared tuple spaces for sensor networks", Proc. of the Euro-American Workshop on Middleware for Sensor Networks, 2006.

76. Nazario, J., "DDoS attack evolution", Network Security, Pp.7-10, 2008.

77. Nelakuditi, S., and Zhang, Z.L., "On selection of paths for multipath routing", Quality of Service-IWQoS, Pp.170-184, 2001.

78. Song, N., Qian, L., and Li, X., "Wormhole attacks detection in wireless ad hoc networks: A statistical analysis approach", 19th IEEE International Parallel and Distributed Processing Symposium, 2005.

79. Liang, O., Sekercioglu, Y.A., and Mani, N., "A survey of multipoint relay based broadcast schemes in wireless ad hoc networks", IEEE Communications Surveys& Tutorials, Vol.8, No.4, Pp.30-46, 2006.

80. Poddar, G.M., and Rastogi, N., "Performance Evaluation of UHCF Using TTL Probing for Packet Spoofing Detection in MANET", Performance Evaluation, Vol.3, No.8, 2014.

81. Poonam, Garg, K., and Misra, M., "Trust based multi path DSR protocol", Proceedings of Fifth International Conference on Availability, Reliability and Security, Pp.204-209, 2010.

82. Narula, P., Dhurandher, S.K., Misra, S., and Woungang, I., "Security in mobile ad-hoc networks using soft encryption and trust-based multi-path routing", Computer Communications, Vol.31, No.4, Pp.760-769, 2008.

83. Pushpa Lakshmi, R., and Vincent Antony Kumar, A., "A fuzzy based secure QoS routing protocol using ant colony optimization for mobile ad hoc network", Journal of Intelligent and Fuzzy Systems, Vol.27, No.1, Pp.317-329, 2014.

84. Raote, N.S., "Defending Warmhole attack in Wireless Ad hoc Network", IJCSES, Vol.2, No.3, 2011.

85. Rehana, J., "Security of wireless sensor network. Helsinki University of Technology, Helsinki," Technical Report TKK-CSE-B5, 2009.

86. Rodoplu, V., and Meng, T.H., "Minimum energy mobile wireless networks", IEEE Journal on Selected Areas in Communications, Vol.17, No.8, Pp.1333-1344, 1999.

87. Royer, E.M., and Toh, C.K., "A review of current routing protocols for ad hoc mobile wireless networks", Personal Communications, Vol.6, No.2, Pp.46-55, 1999.

88. Sabahi, F., "Impact of Threats on Vehicular Adhoc Network Security", International Journal of Computer Theory & Engineering, Vol.4, No.5, 2012.

89. Sandhiya, D., Sangeetha, K., and Latha, R.S., "Adaptive acknowledgement technique with key exchange mechanism for MANET", International Conference on Electronics and Communication Systems (ICECS), Pp. 1-5, 2014.

90. Sarma, H.K.D., and Kar, A., "Security threats in wireless sensor networks", 40th Annual International on Carnahan Conferences Security Technology, Pp. 243-251.

91. Schurgers, C., and Srivastava, M.B., "Energy efficient routing in wireless sensor networks", Military Communications Conference, MILCOM 2001. Communications for Network-Centric Operations: Creating the Information Force, Vol.1, Pp. 357-361, 2001.

92. Sen, J., "Security and privacy challenges in cognitive wireless sensor networks", arXiv preprint arXiv:1302.2253, 2013.

93. Sharif, L., and Ahmed, M., "The Wormhole Routing Attack in Wireless Sensor Networks (WSN)", JIPS, Vol.6, No.2, Pp.177-184, 2010.

94. Sharma, P., "Trust based secure AODV in MANET", Journal of Global Research in Computer Science, Vol.3, No.6, Pp.107-114, 2012.

95. Sharma, R., Athavale, V.A., and Sharma, P., Intrusion Detection Techniques for Mobile Ad Hoc and Wireless Sensor Networks.

96. Shirkande, S.D., and Vatti, R.A., "ACO based routing algorithms for ad-hoc network (WSN, MANETs): A survey. International Conference on Communication Systems and Network Technologies (CSNT), Pp. 230-235, 2013.

97. Sigiuk, H.I., and Ihbeel, A.A., "Performance evaluation of three MANET protocols on WSN. In Communications, Computers and Applications (MIC-CCA)", International Conference on Mosharaka, Pp. 12-17, 2012.

98. Rathore, J.S., "Survey on intrusion detection and prevention system and proposed cost effective solution using software agent", International Journal of Advanced Research in Computer Science and Electronics Engineering (IJARCSEE), Vol.1, No.3, Pp.9, 2012.

99. Singh, S.K., Singh, M.P., and Singh, D.K., "A survey on network security and attack defense mechanism for wireless sensor networks", International Journal of Computer Trends and Technology, Vol.1, No.2, Pp.9-17, 2011.

100.Stojmenovic, I., "Position-based routing in ad hoc networks", IEEE Communications Magazine, Vol.40, No.7, Pp.128-134.

101.Sun, B., Osborne, L., Xiao, Y., and Guizani, S., "Intrusion detection techniques in mobile ad hoc and wireless sensor networks", IEEE Wireless Communications, Vol.14, No.5, Pp.56-63, 2007.

102.Tanejaa, S., Kushb, A., Makkarc, A., and Bhushand, B., "Power management in mobile ad hoc network", International Transaction Journal of Engineering, Management,&Applied Sciences &Technologies, Vol.2, No.2, Pp.45-53.

103.Tariq, U., Hong, M., and Lhee, K.S., "A comprehensive categorization of DDoS attack and DDoS defense techniques", Advanced Data Mining and Applications, Pp. 1025-1036, 2006.

104.Tarique, M., Tepe, K.E., Adibi, S., and Erfani, S., "Survey of multipath routing protocols for mobile ad hoc networks", Journal of Network and Computer Applications, Vol.32, No.6, Pp.1125-1143, 2009.

105.Timcenko, V., and Stojanovic, M., "Application of Forensic Analysis for Intrusion Detection against DDoS Attacks in Mobile Ad Hoc Networks", Proceedings. Recent Advances in Computer Engineering Series WSEAS International Conference. (No. 7), 2012.

106.Timcenko, V., and Stojanovic, M., "Application of forensic analysis for intrusion detection against DDoS attacks in mobile ad hoc networks", Proc. 1st WSEAS Int. Conf. on Information Technology and Computer Networks (ITCN 2012), Pp. 301-310, 2012.

107.Toh, C.K., "A novel distributed routing protocol to support ad-hoc mobile computing", IEEE Fifteenth Annual International Phoenix Conference on Computers and Communications, Pp. 480-486, 1996.

108.Upfal, E., "An O (log N) deterministic packet-routing scheme", Journal of the ACM (JACM), Vol.39, No.1, Pp.55-70, 1992.

109.Vidhyapathi, C.M., Sundar, S., Pal, H., and Punia, K., "Securing MANET From BlackHole And Worm Hole Attacks", International Journal of Engineering and Technology, Vol.5, No.3, 2013.

110.W. Stallings, "Network and Internetwork Security", New Jersey: Prentice Hall, 1995.

111.Wang L, Zhang L, and Shu Y. Dong, "Multipath source routing in wireless ad hoc networks", Canadian conference on electrical and computer engineering, Vol. 1, Pp. 479–83, 2000.

112.Wang, C.T., Lin, C.H., and Chang, C.C., "Threshold signature schemes with traceable signers in group communications", Computer Communications, Vol.21, No.8, Pp.771-776, 1994.

113.WANG, P.D., and CHEN, C.Y., "Security Analysis and Modeling of Mobile Agent Based on WSN" Communications Technology, 12, 050, 2009.

114.Wisitpongphan, N., and O.K. Tonguz, "Disjoint multipath source routing in ad hoc networks: transport capacity", Proceedings of the IEEE 58th vehicular technology conference (VTC), Vol. 4, Pp. 2207–11, 2003.

115.Wu, F.J., Kao, Y.F., and Tseng, Y.C., "From wireless sensor networks towards cyber physical systems", Pervasive and Mobile Computing, Vol.7, No.4, Pp.397-413, 2011.

116.Wu, J., Chen, H., Lou, W., Wang, Z., and Wang, Z., "Label-based DV-HOP localization against wormhole attacks in wireless sensor networks", Fifth International Conference on Networking, Architecture and Storage (NAS), Pp. 79-88, 2010.

117.Wu, T.S., and Hsu, C.L., "Threshold signature scheme using self-certified public keys", Journal of Systems and Software, Vol.67, No.2, Pp.89-97, 2003.

118.Xu, Y., Chen, G., Ford, J., and Makedon, F., "Detecting wormhole attacks in wireless sensor networks", Critical infrastructure protection, Pp. 267-279, 2007.

119.Yang, Z.Y., Juhn, L.S., and Tseng, L.M., "On optimal broadcasting scheme for popular video service", IEEE Transactions on Broadcasting, Vol.45, No.3, Pp.318-322, 1999.

120.Yick, J., Mukherjee, B., and Ghosal, D., "Wireless sensor network survey", Computer networks, Vol.52, No.12, Pp.2292-2330, 2008.

121.Zafar, H., Harle, D., Andonovic, I., and Khawaja, Y., "Performance evaluation of shortest multipath source routing scheme", Communications, IET, Vol.3, No.5, Pp.700-713, 2009.

122.Zhang, K., "Threshold proxy signature schemes", Information Security, Pp. 282-290, 1998.

123.Zhang, Y., Lee, W., and Huang, Y.A., "Intrusion detection techniques for mobile wireless networks", Wireless Networks, Vol.9, No.5, Pp.545-556, 2003.

124.Zhu, J., Qiao, C., and Wang, X., "A comprehensive minimum energy routing scheme for wireless ad hoc networks", Twenty-third Annual Joint Conference of the IEEE Computer and Communications Societies, Vol. 2, Pp. 1437-1445, 2004.

125.Znaidi, W., Minier, M., and Babau, J.P., "An ontology for attacks in wireless sensor networks", 2008.

Publications

1. J. Viji Gripsy and Anna Saro Vijendran, "A Survey on Security Analysis of Routing Protocols", Global Journal of Computer Science & Technology, Vol.11, No.1, Pp.19-24, April 2011.

2. "Analysis of Security Attacks on Mobile Ad hoc Networks", International Seminar On Recent Trends in IT, Kaamadhenu arts and Science college, 11th January 2011.

3. J. Viji Gripsy and Anna Saro Vijendran, " A Survey on Security Schemes for Multipath DSR routing", International Journal of Scientific & Engineering Research, Vol.4, No.5, Pp. 2263-2267,May 2013.

4. J. Viji Gripsy and Anna Saro Vijendran, "Scalable & Secured Route Discovery Mechanism using DSR Protocol", European Journal of Scientific Research, Vol.101, No.2, Pp.177-184, May 2013.

5. J. Viji Gripsy and Anna Saro Vijendran, "QUAD Based Secured Multipath Routing Protocol for Mobile Ad hoc Networks", Information Technology Journal, Vol.13, No.8, Pp.1505-1513, March 2014.

6. J. Viji Gripsy and Anna Saro Vijendran, "A Meticulous Investigation Of Impersonation Attacks On MANETS Using Different Routing Protocols", International Journal of Computer Engineering and Applications, Vol.5, No.1, Pp.106-113, Jan 2014.

7. J. Viji Gripsy and Anna Saro Vijendran, "RECT Zone based Location-Aided Routing for Mobile Adhoc and Sensor Networks", Asian Journal of Scientific Research, Vol.7, No.4, Pp.472-481, June 2014.

8. J. Viji Gripsy and Anna Saro Vijendran, "Performance Evaluation of ASMR With QRS and RZLSR Routing Scheme in Mobile Ad-Hoc &Sensor Networks", International Journal of Future Generation Communication & Networking, Vol.7, No.6, Pp.43-47, 2014.

9. "Enhanced Secure Multipath Routing Scheme In Mobile Adhoc And Sensor Networks", 2nd International Conference On Current Trends In Engineering And Technology, Akshaya College Of Engineering And Technology, 7th&8th July 2014.

10. "Evaluation of Adaptability between Quad and RZLSR Routing Scheme in MASNET", International Conference on Advances in Computing, Electronics and Electrical Technology August 02-03 2014, Kuala Lumpur, Malaysia.

Abbreviations

NAME	ABBREVIATION
ACO	Ant Colony Optimization
AODV	Ad-hoc On-demand Distance Vector
ASMR	Adaptive Secure Multipath Routing
BS	Base Station
CBR	Constant Bit Rate
CH	Cluster Head
CH	Cluster Heads
CPS	Cloud Platform And Systems
CTS	Clear To Send
CWSN	Cognitive Wireless Sensor Networks
DES	Data Encryption Standard
DMPR	Dynamic Multipath Routing Protocol
DoS	Denial of Service
DSR	Dynamic Source Routing
EAACK	Enhanced Adaptive Acknowledgment
EARTH	Efficient Architecture for Running TH reads
FEC	Forward Error Correction
HCF	Hop Count Filter
IDS	Intrusion Detection Systems
IoT	Internet of Things
LAR	Location Aided Routing
MAC	Medium Access Control
MANET	Mobile Ad hoc Networks
MASNET	Mobile Ad-hoc and Sensor Networks
MIMO	Multiple Input Multiple Output
M-MPR	Meshed Multipath Routing

MPR	Multi Point Relay
MRA	Misbehaviour Report Authentication
MRI	Wireless Sensor Networks
NC	Network Controller
NoC	Network on Chip
PDA	Personal Digital Assistant
PDR	Packet Delivery Ratio
QRS	Quadrant Based Routing
RREP	Route Reply
RREQ	Route Request
RSA	Rivest-Shamir-Adleman
RTS	Request To Send
RZLSR	Location Specific Routing
SDC	Shared Distribution Center
SecMR	Secure Multipath Routing Protocol
SeMuRAMAS	Secure Multipath Routing Algorithm for Mobile and Sensor Networks
SF	Selective Forwarding
SMS	Shortest Multipath Source
SND	Secure Neighbour Discovery
SPT	Security, Privacy and Trust
UANET	Underwater Ad-Hoc Networks
UHCF	Updated Hop Count Filtering
UWB	Ultra Wideband
UWSN	Underwater Sensor Networks
VANET	Vehicular Ad-hoc Network
WA	Watchdog Alert
WC	Watchdog Confirmation